Josephine Clay:
Pioneer Horsewoman of the Bluegrass

Josephine Clay:

Pioneer Horsewoman of the Bluegrass

By Henry Clay Simpson, Jr.

Harmony House Publishers–Louisville

Harmony House Publishers
P.O. Box 90
Prospect, KY 40059
502-228-2010

Design: Laura Lee

Printed in the USA

ISBN: 1-56469-125-X

Library of Congress Number: 2005922109

Contents

Illustrations .vi

Preface and Acknowledgements .ix

Prologue .xiii

Selected Genealogy of the Clay and Russell Families .xvi

Part I: Josephine Russell Travels with Her Father

Chapter 1. A Visit to Ashland, the Estate of Henry Clay .3

Chapter 2. Travels to California and Mexico .10

Chapter 3. Romance in Monterey .20

Part II: Mrs. Eugene Erwin

Chapter 4. Erwin Family Life .31

Chapter 5. Tragedy at Vicksburg .42

Part III: Josephine Clay, Horsewoman of the Bluegrass

Chapter 6. John M. Clay .55

Chapter 7. Owner, Manager and Writer .72

Chapter 8. Family Legacy .80

Epilogue .91

Chronology of the Life of Josephine Clay .97

Selections from the Writing of Josephine Clay .101

a. "Who Rode La Sylphide?" *The Sport of Kings: Racing Stories* (New York, 1912)

b. "Sue Munday," *Frank Logan: A Novel* (New York, 1901)

c. Selected Poetry, *Lexington Herald*, 1902–1905

d. Note from the 1899 "Annual Catalogue of Brood Mares"

List of Illustrations

0.1 Signature Collection in the Scrapbook of Josephine Clay. *UK*

0.2 Letter from President Abraham Lincoln to John M. Clay, August 9, 1862. *UK*

1.1 Henry Clay by Lafosse

1.2 Ashland by James Hamilton

1.3 Note from Henry Clay to Josephine Russell, 1843. *UK*

1.4 Ashland Stock Book. *UK*

2.1 Map of the California Trail and the Hastings Cutoff. *National Park Service*

2.2 Indian Medicine Bag Owned by Josephine Russell

2.3 Mexican Visa Obtained by Colonel Russell in Acapulco, 1850. *UK*

2.4 Mexican Silver Spoon Presented to Josephine by Francisco Ramiro, June 1851

3.1 The Old Customs House at Monterey, California. *California State Parks*

3.2 Josephine Deborah Russell

3.3 Andrew Eugene Erwin

4.1 The Woodlands, the Erwin Home in Lexington. *J. Winston Coleman Kentuckiana Collection, Transylvania University*

4.2 Guards Pass from the Command of Brig. Gen. James C. Veatch, April 3, 1863. *UK*

5.1 Map of the Civil War Fighting Near Vicksburg. *U. S. Army Military Historical Institute*

5.2 Underground Houses in Vicksburg, June 1863. *Vicksburg National Military Park*

5.3 Col. Eugene Erwin

5.5 Monument to Col. Eugene Erwin. *Vicksburg National Military Park*

5.6 Josephine Erwin's Request for Spits Camphor. *UK*

5.7 Mrs. Eugene Erwin

5.8 Gen. Ulysses S. Grant, 1863. *Library of Congress*

5.9 Pass to Independence, Missouri, for "Mrs. Col. Erwin" Signed by General Grant. *UK*

5.10 Note from Custis Washington, Chief of Steamer Imperial, July 23, 1863. *UK*

5.11 Order of Protection from Maj. Gen. John M. Schofield, November 3, 1863. *UK*

6.1 John M. Clay

6.2 *Star Davis* at Ashland Stock Farm by Thomas J. Scott, 1856

6.3 Pedigree Wheel for *Star Davis*

6.4 *Skedaddle* and *Squeeze'em* by Thomas J. Scott, 1869

6.5 Racing Purses Won by Ashland Stock Farm

6.6 Mr. and Mrs. John M. Clay

6.7 Monument to John M. Clay at the Lexington Cemetery

7.1 Josephine Clay Pictured with "Friends" in *Frank Logan. The Abbey Press*

7.2 The 1899 "Annual Catalogue of Brood Mares" for Ashland Stock Farm

7.3 Josephine Clay and Grooms with *La Sylphide, Buff and Blue*, and *Bonnet o'Blue* at Ashland on Tates Creek Pike. *Turf, Field & Farm*, 1899

7.4 W. T. Woodard Catalogue of Sales, November 1903. *Keeneland Association Library*

8.1 Minor Simpson

8.2 Lucretia Erwin

8.3 Josephine Clay in Her Study at Ashland on Tates Creek Road

8.4 Battle Flag of the Sixth Missouri Infantry CSA. *Wood Simpson*

8.5 Josephine Clay with Family at Ashland on Tates Creek Road, 1900

8.6 Invitation to "Fête-champêtre." *UK*

8.7 Victor Bogaret to Josephine Clay, March 22, 1919. *UK*

9.1 Henry Clay Simpson and his mother, Lucretia Erwin Simpson, with the Ice Houses of Ashland in the Background

9.2 Map of Chevy Chase, Lexington, Kentucky showing the location of Ashland Stock Farm (left), the additional acreage purchased by John M. Clay (middle) and the Pettit Farm purchased by Josephine Clay (right). *Prepared by William A. LaBach*

Tables

1. The Ten Most Successful Horses Bred by Josephine Clay

2. Josephine Clay's Property Transactions in Central Kentucky

Unless otherwise noted, all documents and photographs used as illustrations or referenced in the text are the property of the author's family. Josephine Clay's scrapbook and collection of Clay family documents were donated in 2004 to the University of Kentucky Libraries (*UK*).

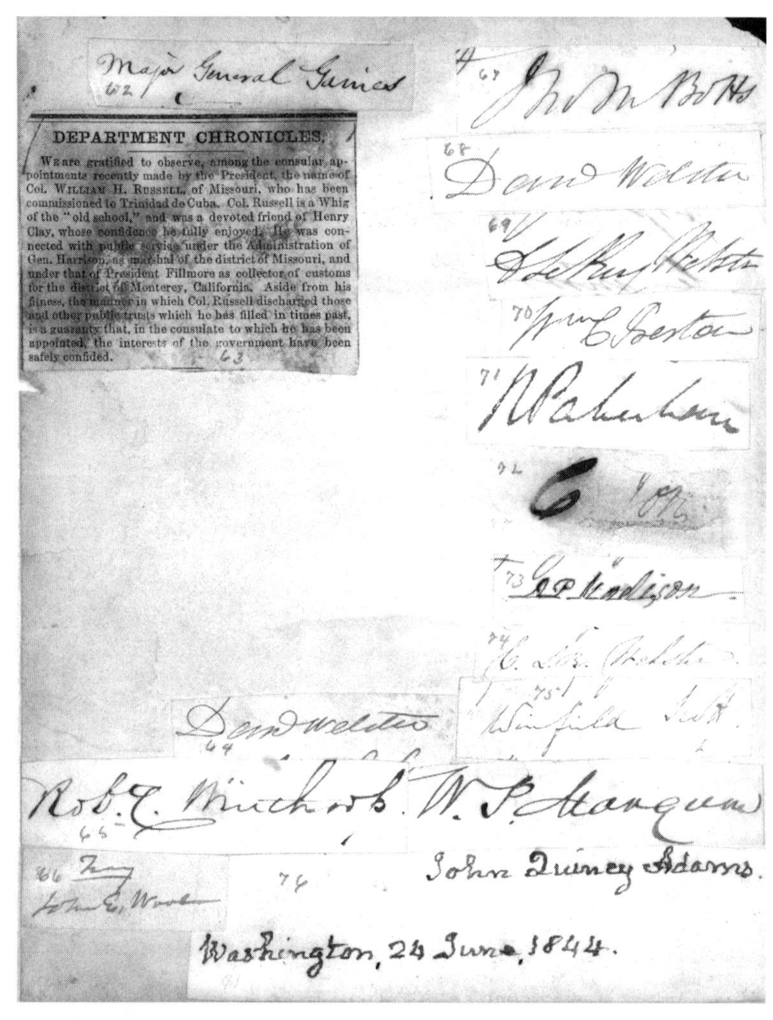

DEPARTMENT CHRONICLES.

We are gratified to observe, among the consular appointments recently made by the President, the name of Col. William H. Russell, of Missouri, who has been commissioned to Trinidad de Cuba. Col. Russell is a Whig of the "old school," and was a devoted friend of Henry Clay, whose confidence he fully enjoyed. He was connected with public service under the Administration of Gen. Harrison, as marshal of the district of Missouri, and under that of President Fillmore as collector of customs for the district of Monterey, California. Aside from his fitness, the manner in which Col. Russell discharged those and other public trusts which he has filled in times past, is a guaranty that, in the consulate to which he has been appointed, the interests of the government have been safely confided.

Fig. 0.1 Signature Collection in the Scrapbook of Josephine Clay.[1] *UK*

Preface and Acknowledgements

My trip to Lexington, Kentucky, in early March 2003 began with a surprise. The worst ice storm anyone could remember limited movement around the town as trees were removed from the roads. My mother, now in her nineties, and I were housebound in her older home filled with family papers and artifacts. In her downstairs bedroom, I sat looking out a window at her frozen garden. On the table next to my chair, I saw an old leather-bound scrapbook stamped in gold "Mrs. John M. Clay." Mrs. Clay was my great-grandmother whose full name was Josephine Russell Erwin Clay.

Skimming through the thick volume, I saw a "signature collection" with several people I recognized from American history: Daniel Webster, Dolly P. Madison, Winfield Scott, John Quincy Adams, and Robert C. Winthrop.

I read a letter from President Abraham Lincoln to John M. Clay, youngest son of Henry Clay, the nineteenth-century U. S. senator and presidential candidate from Kentucky. Ten years after his father's death, as the Civil War fighting intensified, John Clay sent his father's silver snuffbox to Lincoln with a note. He told Lincoln that he agreed with his father "that he owed a higher allegiance to the constitution and government of the United States than to the government of any state . . . ." He received a quick response.

Executive Mansion
Washington, August 9, 1862

Mr. John M. Clay.

My dear Sir:

The Snuff-box you sent, with the accompanying note, was received yesterday.

Thanks for this memento of your great and patriotic father. Thanks also for the assurance that, in these days of dereliction, you remain true to his principles. In the concurrent sentiment of your venerable mother, so long the partner of his bosom and his honors, and lingering now, where he was, but for the call to rejoin him where he is, I recognize his voice, speaking as it ever spoke, for the Union, the Constitution, and the freedom of mankind.

Your Obt. Servt.
[Obedient Servant]
A. Lincoln[2]

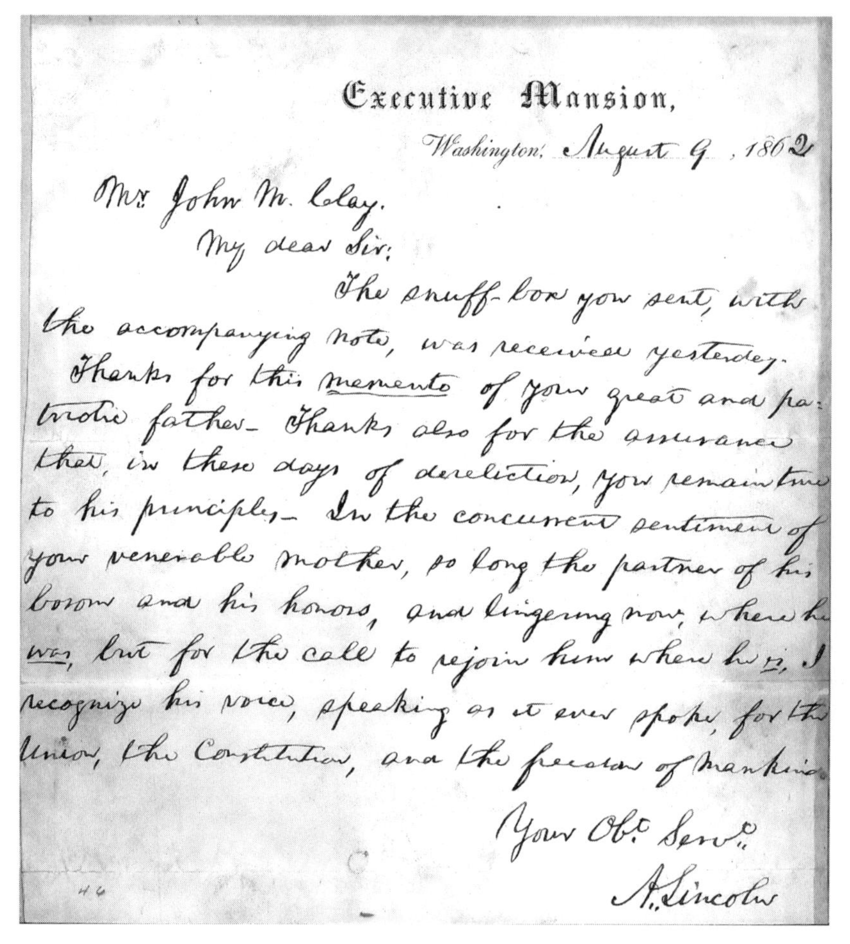

Executive Mansion,
Washington, August 9, 1862

Mr. John M. Clay.

My dear Sir:

The snuff-box you sent, with the accompanying note, was received yesterday.

Thanks for this memento of your great and patriotic father– Thanks also for the assurance that, in these days of dereliction, you remain true to his principles– In the concurrent sentiment of your venerable mother, so long the partner of his bosom and his honors, and lingering now, where he was, but for the call to rejoin him where he is, I recognize his voice, speaking as it ever spoke, for the Union, the Constitution, and the freedom of mankind.

Your Obt. Servt.
A. Lincoln

Fig. 0.2 Letter from President Abraham Lincoln to John M. Clay, August, 1862. *UK*

My great-grandmother's scrapbook contains over 150 pages of articles, letters, and poems spanning her life from 1835 to 1920. Documents were pasted into the scrapbook randomly, so I prepared a chronology of events and a list of the places she visited.

At the age of seven, my great-grandmother traveled with her father, Col. William H. Russell, from their home on the frontier in Missouri to Washington, D. C. During the return trip, they visited White Sulphur Springs, Virginia, and Ashland, the estate of Henry Clay in Lexington, Kentucky. She visited Washington again with her father when she was eleven. The former First Lady, Dolly P. Madison, copied an Elizabethan poem, "Truth," into the child's scrapbook during the trip.[3]

When Josephine was thirteen, she traveled west with her father on a gold rush wagon train to Monterey, California. I learned that they also visited Mexico when I found a poem addressed to "Miss Josephine" by a family friend on board the steamship *Alabama* near Acapulco.

For two years Josephine and her father lived in the old Monterey Customs House on the bay. Josephine's scrapbook contains the calling cards of early Californians, including Capt. Douglas Ottinger of the U. S. Revenue Cutter, *Frolic.* The forty-eight-year-old married captain became infatuated with Josephine, and for eighteen months he visited and corresponded with her. But when she met Eugene Erwin, the young grandson of Henry Clay who arrived in Monterey, she fell in love. With the strong encouragement of her father, Josephine accepted Eugene's proposal of marriage, and the couple returned to the Missouri frontier. Eugene wanted to develop a career as a merchant supplying gold rush caravans.

My sister, who was named for her great-grandmother, saved an old photograph of Josephine when she was sixteen, water stained with the sepia fading. A photographic laboratory scanned and restored the image to its original color and form. The result was a strong, attractive-looking young woman with dark hair and eyes, dressed in silk, with a holy cross pendant and heavy earrings, her hands posed for a classic portrait. As I learned more about her, I came back to this image again and again, and began to see an inner strength that allowed her to live an adventurous, independent life beyond the constraints of the Victorian era.

The scrapbook also contains letters and documents from the Civil War campaign in Mississippi. My great-grandmother was described as "Mrs. Col. Eugene Erwin" during her service as a nurse at the siege of Vicksburg. Her husband was killed on June 25, 1863 leading a counterattack against an assault by the Union troops of Gen. Ulysses S. Grant. I found his obituary in the scrapbook, printed on a ten-inch yellow ribbon distributed to the Southern defenders. A note written by General Grant authorized my great-grandmother and her nine-year-old daughter to return to their home in Missouri via government transport. The deaths of Josephine's husband and an infant daughter during the Civil War transformed her bright personality; she developed a single-minded dedication to the survival of her family in wartime Missouri. Josephine wrote that she was determined "to paddle my own canoe; and if the craft went down, to sink with her."

When my father was living, he often talked about his grandmother, but his recollections were limited to the period near the end of her life when he lived at her home, "Ashland on Tates Creek Road" in Lexington. To investigate Josephine's life further would require historical research. Though it had been many years since I studied history in college, I looked forward to the challenge. I had been reading *Angle of Repose* by Wallace Stegner, which tells the story of a writer trying to learn more about his grandmother's life and the challenges he faced in searching for information about her early history. He wrote that his research was like listening to a lower and lower-pitched sound of a train moving rapidly away from you—what he called the Doppler effect in studying family history.[4]

I began by corresponding with historians and archivists in Kentucky, Missouri, California, and Mississippi, sending each an outline of Josephine Clay's life and asking for information and suggested references. I received enthusiastic support throughout an eighteen month research effort, especially from the staff at the King Library at the University of Kentucky; Ashland, the estate of Henry Clay; and The Filson Historical Society.

In 1866, my great-grandmother and her family were invited by the Clay family to visit Lexington, Kentucky, and a few months later she married her first husband's uncle, John M. Clay. Together, they managed a small, but very successful Thoroughbred horse farm, Ashland Stock Farm, once part of the estate of Henry Clay. After John Clay's death in 1887, she inherited the farm and immediately began to expand the operation. She increased her property holdings on the Tates Creek Road in Lexington to over a thousand acres and her stock from a dozen broodmares to fifty. When Josephine Clay bred the winner of the Kentucky Derby in 1890, her yearlings brought record prices at the horse sales in New York, and she became the subject of articles about her success in the national press. A history of racing for this period described her as "the only woman in the United States engaged in this particular kind of business . . . she was not less successful than her husband had been in raising some distinguished performers for the turf and in adding value to the blood of the American race horse."[5]

While managing the horse farm, she began a second career writing articles and popular novels. I found Josephine Clay's novels at the University of Kentucky Libraries.[6] Her writing is autobiographical and describes women who overcome setbacks in their lives and are successful in working careers. The strong female characters are farm managers, jockeys, horse trainers, even military leaders and lion trainers. To illustrate a story of her life, I used examples of her writing and, wherever possible, my great-grandmother's words.

I am indebted to the following people who read the manuscript and provided valuable advice, assistance and research information: William J. Marshall, Director of Special Collections and Archives, Dr. James D. Birchfield, and Claire McCann of the King Library at the University of Kentucky; William Cooke, Director of the International Museum of the Kentucky Horse Park; Dr. Lindsey Apple, former Chairman of the History Department at Georgetown College; Dr. Melba Porter Hay, former Division Manager for Research & Publications, Kentucky Historical Society; Eric Brooks, Curator of Ashland, the Estate of Henry Clay; Sue Andrew, member of the Board of the Henry Clay Memorial Foundation; William Anderson LaBach, an attorney and descendant of Josephine Clay, and his wife, Karen LaBach; Cathy C. Schenck, Director of the Keeneland Association Library; Kent M. Brown, an attorney and Civil War writer; Anne Peters of Three Chimneys Farm; and James J. Holmberg, Curator of Special Collections at The Filson Historical Society. I also want to thank Dr. Thomas H. Appleton, Professor of History at Eastern Kentucky University, for editorial assistance.

Research information and photographs were also provided by historians and archivists at the following organizations: California State Parks (Sacramento, California), J. Winston Coleman Kentuckiana Collection, Transylvania University (Lexington, Kentucky), Jackson County Historical Society (Independence, Missouri), Kingdom of Callaway County Historical Society (Fulton, Missouri), The Ulysses S. Grant Association, Southern Illinois University (Carbondale, Illinois), U. S. Army Military History Institute (Carlisle, Pennsylvania), U. S. Coast Guard Historian's Office (Washington, D. C.), and the Vicksburg National Military Park (Vicksburg, Mississippi).

I received encouragement and assistance from my family—especially my wife, Kitty Simpson; nephew, Hart Simpson; daughters, Kate Simpson, Anne Clay Paumgarten, and Josephine Clay Simpson; sons-in-law, Michael Burgmaier and Alexander Paumgarten; brother, Wood Simpson; and sister, Josephine Russell Simpson. This book is dedicated to my mother, Louisiana Wood Simpson, who first encouraged me to read Josephine's scrapbook.

Clay Simpson
December, 2004

Prologue

The community of Lexington, Kentucky, was carved from Indian hunting territory in the 1780s in large part by pioneers migrating west from Virginia. It grew rapidly to become the largest town west of the Allegheny Mountains, known for the beauty of its rolling countryside, the fertility of its soil, and its bountiful crops of hemp, tobacco, and wheat. For a time, it was the center of frontier trade. By 1800, there were 1,795 inhabitants, of whom 23 were Indians and 439 slaves.[1]

In 1797, a young lawyer who would become Lexington's most famous resident arrived from Hanover County, Virginia. Henry Clay, the celebrated nineteenth century statesman, was barely twenty years old when he followed his mother and her new husband to Lexington to practice law. About six feet tall, dynamic, and entertaining with a sharp wit, he could swear, drink, and gamble with the best of the local men. He quickly achieved a reputation for settling land disputes and winning acquittals for his clients in criminal cases with persuasive stories and anecdotes.

Henry Clay's career accelerated after 1799, when he married Lucretia Hart, the daughter of a prominent early settler, Thomas Hart. Clay was elected to the Kentucky state legislature in 1803, and five years later served as the Speaker of the Kentucky House. He attracted large crowds in Kentucky with entertaining speeches about the potential for western development and became known as "Harry of the West" and the "Great Orator."[2]

Chosen by the state legislature to complete two short, unexpired terms in the United States Senate, Clay established himself as a leader of the western states by pushing for western development and expansion. In 1810, he was elected by the Kentucky voters to the more lively and powerful U. S. House of Representatives and identified with the "war hawks" who increasingly advocated war with England. On his first day in office in November 1811, Clay was voted the Speaker of the House by a two-to-one margin.

War with England was declared in 1812, followed by an unsuccessful invasion of Canada by an American fighting force and a British invasion of the U. S. mainland. Two years later the fighting reached a standstill, and the U. S. Treasury was depleted. It was clear that the nation was not prepared for a protracted struggle. Clay tried to rally Congress to support the War, but after two years of conflict, both countries were ready for peace. President James Madison appointed Clay a Peace Commissioner, and he traveled with John Quincy Adams to Belgium to negotiate a treaty. After the commissioners successfully signed the Treaty of Ghent with England, Clay traveled to London and Paris and "hobnobbed" with royalty, acquiring a new nickname in Kentucky—"Prince Hal."

The popular and ambitious Clay ran for president in 1824. When none of the five candidates obtained an electoral majority, the election was thrown to the House of Representatives, where Clay helped John Quincy Adams defeat Gen. Andrew Jackson. Adams subsequently appointed Clay as his Secretary of State, leading to charges of a "corrupt bargain" by General Jackson and his supporters.

Fig. 1.1 Henry Clay by Lafosse

In the following presidential election of 1828, Jackson's victory over Adams was a blow to Clay's ambition to become president as he was no longer the undisputed leader of the western states. When Clay heard that Jackson had won the election in Kentucky, he was humiliated and tired. He returned to Ashland, his estate in Lexington, and at age fifty-one, announced his retirement from public affairs.

Clay spent the following winter in New Orleans with his family. He found support during his trip to encourage him to reconsider his retirement. But he needed to regain national attention. His supporters lobbied for his election to the U. S. Senate from Kentucky to establish a platform for a return to national politics.

To be elected to the U. S. Senate, Clay had to win the combined vote of the two branches of the Kentucky state legislature against Richard M. Johnson, a Jackson supporter. But he had not gauged the strong support for President Jackson. The vote in the Kentucky Senate gave nineteen votes to Johnson and eighteen for Clay. A defeat in his own state would signal to the world that Clay's announced retirement from politics would be permanent. His best hope was to rally support in the Kentucky House.

Attention began to focus on William Henry Russell, the youngest member of the Kentucky House of Representatives at age twenty-nine. Russell was a large man, six feet one inch tall, with an ego to match. He was a popular representative from Nicholas County, a hilly section north of Lexington, with a bombastic style of speaking that had been effective in gaining notoriety. But his family's influence extended beyond his constituency. Russell's grandfather, William Russell, had served as brigadier general in George Washington's Grand Army of the Republic, and his family was prominent among the early Virginia settlers of Lexington.[3] He was married to Zaenett

Freeland, an attractive, well educated woman from Baltimore's prominent Freeland family, an important connection for the young lawyer.

William H. Russell studied law at Transylvania College in Lexington, where Henry Clay was a professor of law. After graduation, he served as a clerk to Clay, where he developed an allegiance to the man he called Prince Hal. Russell wrote to Clay on December 9, 1830, saying that he would support his election to the U. S. Senate but would be forced to leave his office as a result:

> [I] received from my county the signatures of about four hundred of my constituents instructing me to vote for a Jackson senator, or be turned out of office. . . .this determination will cause me almost immediately to expatriate myself, for Nicholas will be by far too hot for me, I shall be placed in a most dreadful situation, too unpleasant to remain in the neighborhood of men, who will regard me for the most virtuous & praiseworthy act of my life, a traitor and deceiver—yes, I will leave them.[4]

Clay's allies began to marshal their support in the Kentucky House. In the final House vote in 1831, Clay overcame the deficit in the Kentucky Senate and was elected by the combined narrow margin of nine votes. Clay was upset with the close vote in his home state and said "I go to my post . . . . with no anticipation of pleasure from occupying it."[5] Russell claimed to his friends that he made the difference in Clay's election.[6] He was determined to gain a political job and a steady income for his assistance.

In the Senate, Henry Clay became one of the three senators known as the "great triumvirate." Clay, John C. Calhoun, and Daniel Webster dominated a powerful Senate that shaped the country's public policy for the next twenty years. His entertaining speeches were always reported in the national news. Tall, slender, often wearing a black dress coat that contrasted with his white hair, his face was bright, playful, and grinning as his voice rang through the Senate Chamber with strong criticism of President Andrew Jackson.[7]

Selected Genealogy of the Clay and Russell Families

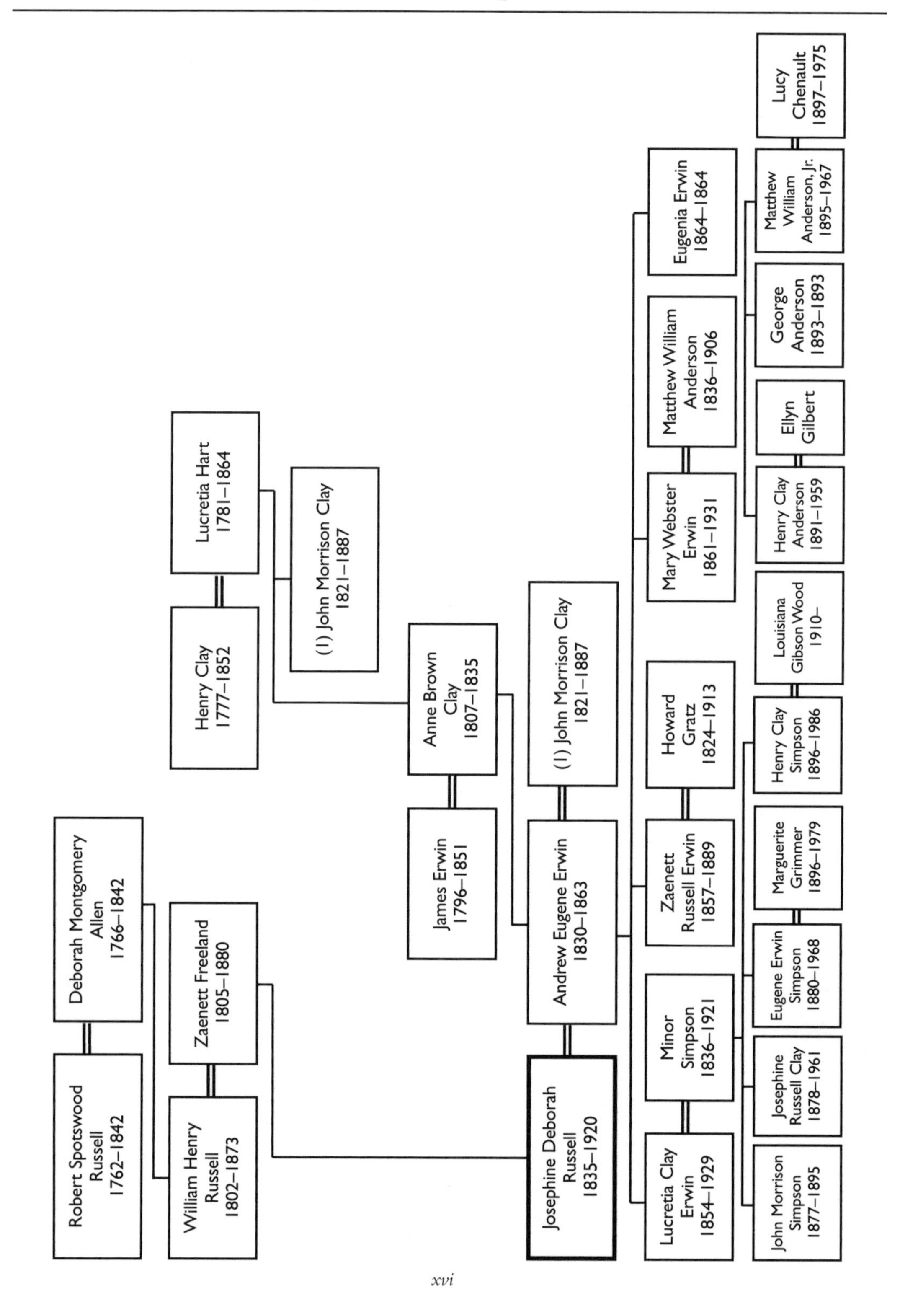

Part I

Josephine Russell Travels with Her Father

Chapter 1

A Visit to Ashland, the Estate of Henry Clay

The corn for the reaper is ready and waiting. Fruits of the orchards ripe for the taking.[1]

The Russell family moved from Virginia to the bluegrass area of Kentucky in the 1780s to claim a two-thousand-acre land grant from the state of Virginia. Brig. Gen. William Russell, who served in George Washington's Grand Army of the Republic, had given the property jointly to his sons, William and Robert. It was located six miles north of Lexington on a small country lane that was later named the Russell Cave Pike. The brothers divided the property, with William taking the spring at Russell Cave and a smaller tract closer to Lexington, while Robert assumed the ownership of the tract to the north. The brothers built two palatial residences with construction workers from Virginia and materials transported across the mountains in huge wagons called "land ships." The largest house, built by William, was named "Mount Brilliant" for the estate of Patrick Henry in Virginia; and a smaller Georgian stone house called "Poplar Hill" was constructed by Robert on a high point in a grove of poplar trees, a mile farther out from Lexington. William Henry Russell was born at Poplar Hill in 1802, the son of Robert Spotswood Russell and Deborah Montgomery Russell, the eighth child in a large family of ten children.[2]

A colony of Virginians moved within a few miles—the Harrisons at "Elk Hill," the Merediths at "Winton," and the Breckinridges at "Cabell's Dale," and their social gatherings were frequent and enlivened by impromptu dances and other amusements.[3] "The Russell family practiced hospitality according to the Scottish maxim: foster your guest so long as he wishes to stay. Cousins by the dozens visited from Virginia, and it was said that no wayfarer seeking lodging was ever turned away."[4] They had "indelibly stamped on their foreheads the cabalistic letters F. F.V. [First Families of Virginia] and no expense was spared in upholding their status."[5]

After living in central Kentucky for a generation, the Russell family decided to seek new opportunities on the frontier in Missouri. They were highly regarded for leadership in the local legislature and the Kentucky militia, but the family's income from crops and a small distillery on their property was not sufficient to cover the expenses of their lifestyle and a growing family.

For the third time in three generations, the Russell family sold their property and acquired cheaper land on the frontier. They previously lived in Culpeper County, Virginia, from 1734 and moved to the Clinch River area in southwestern Virginia during the Revolutionary War.[6] After the war, the Russell family migrated to central Kentucky. On October 5, 1831, William H. Russell led the family's third move west to a small frontier community located near Fulton, Missouri, formed by a group of transplanted Virginians and Kentuckians. They built comfortable homes on high bluffs above the Missouri River about sixty miles upstream from St. Louis.[7]

Zaenett Russell wrote to her mother urging her to join them in Missouri. In a letter dated December 11, 1836, she said: "you have no idea how comfortable and happy all of our cousins are. It looks like old Fayette . . .so many here, old Uncle Freeland looks as much at home as if he was raised here, his family rides in an elegant barouche and all the cousins have fine carriages . . .a style of living [that] would be considered first rate anywhere . . . ."[8] This was in contrast to the experience reported for most of the settlers in the area who depended on hardscrabble farming, hunting, and fishing.[9]

On December 7, 1835, William and Zaenett Russell had their fifth child and only daughter, Josephine Deborah Russell. The Russell family continued to grow, and she would have six brothers.[10] As a child she was mature for her age, tall and tom-boyish looking with dark hair and eyes—not pretty, but an attractive, outgoing girl who was popular with her brothers and her father. She wrote that she enjoyed competing with her brothers in the rough frontier games of horse racing, fencing, and shooting.[11]

Josephine and her brothers received a home education. She later recalled:

> There was in town, a French priest, accomplished and learned—indeed, his bishop had plainly told him that too much learning had made him mad and inclined him to unauthorized views, and since he refused either to retract or to hold his tongue, he was forbidden to celebrate the mass. Debarred this privilege, a priest seems singularly out of place in the world—a goose straying on a turnpike is not more helpless. But there is a silver lining to most clouds, and the priest, yet not a priest, found support and occupation in teaching the Colonel's children; he even taught music [and Josephine learned to play the banjo and piano]. And she shared the lessons of her brothers in the use of firearms, and fencing—and perhaps to the foils she was somewhat indebted for the beauty, ease and firmness of her poses.[12]

Josephine's father liked to sing early American songs and invited his daughter at an early age to travel with him and help entertain his guests by playing the banjo or piano while he sang.[13] He called her "Joe," which became her nickname. According to a publisher's biographical note that my great-grandmother probably wrote, she said that "in her girlhood, she accompanied her father on various excursions, so that she began to see and understand life almost as soon as she opened her eyes."[14]

In 1836, Russell volunteered for the local militia to fight in the Seminole Indian War in Florida. After a successful action against an Indian tribe that refused to be relocated, he returned as Colonel and Judge Advocate of the Missouri militia and was elected to the Missouri legislature. Thereafter, he was known as "Colonel" Russell.[15]

Russell tried to develop a legal practice for Kentuckians who wanted to invest in land in Missouri, but he told his older brother Thomas, who stayed in Kentucky, that he was unsuccessful in finding clients.[16] He campaigned for Whig Party candidates and urged Henry Clay to visit Missouri, but the senator responded that he would "make no visits except as required by health or business."[17]

An opportunity for gaining a government appointment came in the 1840 presidential election. Colonel Russell was selected to be a member of the Whig National Convention that nominated Gen. William Henry Harrison for president, and he actively campaigned for Harrison throughout Missouri. When Harrison was elected, Russell, with Henry Clay's support, finally obtained the appointment he had been seeking since 1831. On July 26, 1841, Daniel Webster, Secretary of State

Fig. 1.2 Ashland by James Hamilton

for President Harrison, named Russell the U. S. marshal for Missouri and the adjacent Indian territories (Kansas, Nebraska, and Iowa).[18] With a staff of assistant marshals, he was responsible for the collection of federal taxes, administering the U. S. census and enforcing Federal laws including the transport of criminals wanted in other states. He became well known for sponsoring legislation to establish a Circuit and District Court in Missouri to enforce Federal laws. But he complained that the job was "unprofitable" and lobbied with key members of Congress for an increase in the pay for U. S. marshals.[19] He served as U. S. marshal for only two years until a new president, John Tyler, was elected. Russell's job was threatened by Tyler's need to appoint his own representative in Missouri, and he again looked to Henry Clay to help him obtain a new position.

In July 1843, Clay received a note from Colonel Russell indicating the date his family would arrive in Lexington. He immediately asked Mrs. Clay to invite the Russell family to dine at the Clay home, Ashland, one mile east of the town. Colonel Russell would be staying with his brother Thomas and his family at Ash Hill north of Lexington, near his birthplace.

Lexington had fallen well behind the Ohio River cities of Louisville and Cincinnati in commercial development and population growth, yet maintained its position as the center of education and social life in Kentucky with many prominent visitors to the beautiful estates surrounding the town. Of all the large southern-style mansions in the Bluegrass, Ashland was the favorite of visitors. Henry Clay and his wife, Lucretia, were especially gracious hosts and took pride in showing their guests the unusual specimens of trees, plants, and livestock on the farm.

Colonel and Mrs. Russell and their seven-year-old daughter, Josephine, arrived by carriage at noon, traveling on the dusty road that was a continuation of the main street of Lexington. Two roughly hewn square posts, shaded by tall locust trees, marked the entrance to Ashland. Moments later they were joined by Colonel Russell's brother, Thomas, and his wife, Sarah, and the entire Russell family walked up the grass path shaded by an avenue of hemlocks, ashes, and walnuts with foliage interlacing overhead. When the door to the main house opened, they saw an octagonal hall with walls of highly polished walnut and ash cut from trees on the farm. Windows looked out upon a greenhouse and garden in back of the house. On the right was a reception room with a dining room beyond, where Henry and Lucretia Clay welcomed them.[20] The Clay's youngest son, John and grandson, Eugene Erwin, both living at Ashland at this time, joined the party.

Colonel Russell presented Henry Clay with a colorful Indian hunting shirt, a gift from Daniel Boone's grandson, who lived near them in Missouri.[21] As U. S. marshal of the Indian territories, Colonel Russell had an important role in Indian affairs, and a lively discussion ensued about how to promote peace with the tribes.

The Russell family was returning from a trip to Washington, where they met President Tyler. Zaenett had accompanied her husband, and Russell was deeply offended when the president announced in her presence that he planned to replace Russell as U. S. marshal with one of his own supporters. Clay had written to Russell on May 11, 1843:

> I am glad to see that you bear your removal, as I anticipated you would, with scorn and contempt for its author. But really Mrs. Russell . . . has displayed more than Roman spirit in her treatment of that event. I think that Capt. Tyler has placed you under very heavy obligations for the opportunity he has afforded you of enjoying more of the conversation and company of such an estimable wife. I shall be most happy to see you here, and hope you will come; and my satisfaction would be increased if you would bring with you your Lady, whom I have long had reason to esteem and admire . . . .[22]

The Russell's daughter Josephine was surprisingly mature for her age, and with Henry Clay and the other adults, she acted with quiet confidence. But when Clay asked her to sit beside him at the dinner table, she later wrote:

> That she appreciated the honor, but was hardly prepared for it, and felt rather abashed; but "Prince Hal," while entertaining his other guests with that brilliant playfulness which was so remarkable, would drop an occasional word into her ear and attend personally to her plate. She was beginning to feel bland and self-possessed until helped to an artichoke—something she detested—and she could not eat, although politeness seemed to require the sacrifice. In her excited state, the artichoke increased in bulk and she thought it would attract eyes to her discredit. But presto! The great man who had brought the trouble upon her removed it. "So you don't like artichokes," he said. "Why I adore them," and straightway the conical, oval-scaled vegetable was appropriated to his use. When the coffee was brought in, he asked Mrs. Clay if it was some of the Liberian coffee, mentioning with evident satisfaction that a present of several sacks of coffee had been sent to him by the colonists. Henry Clay was president of the American Colonization Society . . . . which encouraged the emancipation of slaves and their return to an independent Republic of Liberia.[23]

When Josephine showed her dining companion an album she was using to record the signature of each person she met, Clay immediately took out a pen and wrote: "I record my name, with great pleasure, in the album of the daughter of one of my best, one of the most faithful and intelligent of my friends."[24]

After dinner, Clay escorted the men to the drawing room, where they probably discussed Clay's plans for next year's presidential campaign in Missouri, while the women and children toured the grounds surrounding Ashland. Josephine later recalled:

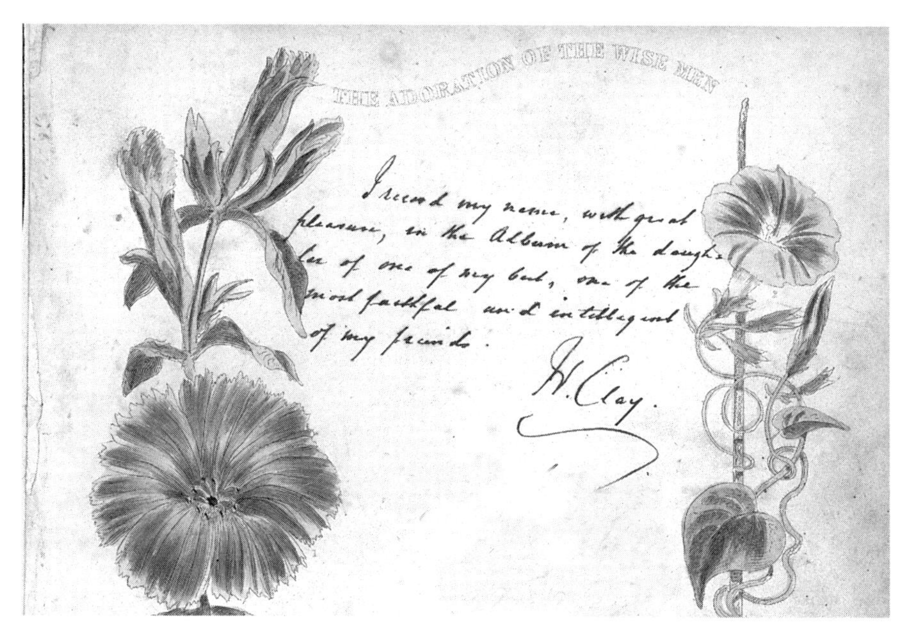

THE ADORATION OF THE WISE MEN

I record my name, with great pleasure, in the Album of the daughter of one of my best, one of the most faithful and intelligent of my friends.

H. Clay.

Fig. 1.3 Note from Henry Clay to Josephine Russell, 1843. *UK*

> The exceeding beauty of a Kentucky stock farm cannot be adequately described when the trees are in the graceful foliage of early summer, the glowing sun, in generous profusion, pouring down the warmth of his golden light all over the living sheen of the luxuriant blue-grass. And beneath the azure sky fresh and fragrant are the breezes [that] wafted over sweet flowers. Within the ten counties distinctively [called] the "Blue Grass Region," there was no lovelier estate.[25]

Lucretia Hart Clay's personality contrasted with her outgoing husband. She was a plain looking woman with very little interest in social affairs. During her husband's long absences in Washington, she focused on raising a large family and managing the Ashland household.[26] While the ladies and Josephine walked the paths surrounding the large house, she described how her husband bought the first acreage in 1804 with a dream of creating an experimental farm that would introduce new types of plants and animals that could be an example to others. At Ashland, she said, he found recreation in planting orchards and gardens with new varieties of shrubs and fruits. Each morning he asked for a favorite flower or fruit, and if a red Luxemburg Rose was in bloom, it would be placed on his breakfast plate.[27]

Ashland's livestock was the finest in the Bluegrass—jacks and jennies from Spain and Malta, pigs from Portugal, new breeds of cattle from England, Merino sheep from Pennsylvania, and in 1830 Henry Clay established one of the area's first Thoroughbred horse breeding farms.[28] In 1835, he purchased the famous broodmare *Allegrante* and several other horses from Gov. James Barbour of Virginia for $1,000.[29] Lucretia showed her guests the Ashland stock book, with her husband's entries. After 1839 her youngest son, John, kept the records for the farm. In the future, Ashland focused on breeding Thoroughbred horses and became one of the most successful horse farms in nineteenth-century America.[30]

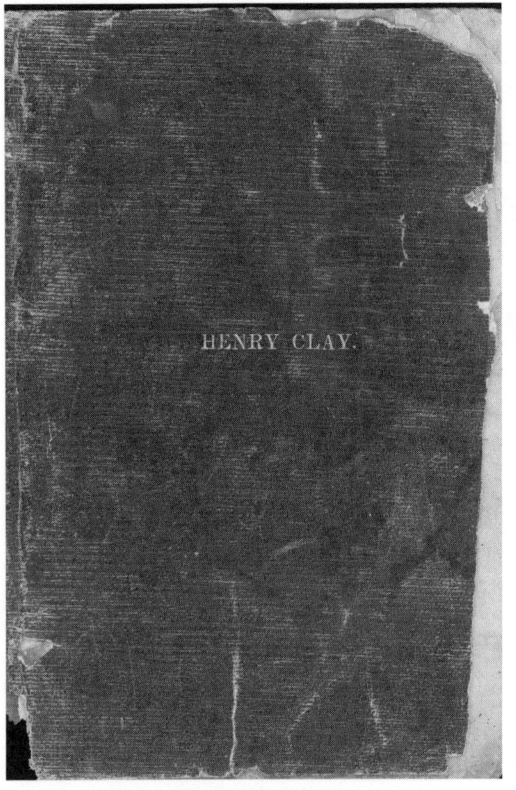

Births in 1865.
Lusby Cow had a spotted heifer calf the 1st of January.
Lusby Cow's heifer had her first calf a red bull the 6th of February.
Madeline had a ch f. by Revenue the 12th March.
Walloon had a b f. by Lexington the 16th March.
Heraldry had a br filly by Austerlitz the 26th March -
Red heifer white face had a red heifer calf 3d April
Barnton mare a sorel filly 14th April Good Friday by Star Davis
Voucher mare had a brown colt 16th April Easter Sunday by Austerlitz
Large roan (almost white) cow had a bull calf the 12th May -
(sold
Bruce cow had a red + white heifer calf 7th June
Small half Alderney 3 yr old roan cow had a light roan bull calf 10th June sold
Dark red heifer had her first calf a red heifer the 24th June sold
Shelby cow had a red bull calf the 20th November
Lusby cow had a calf the 22d December

Fig. 1.4 Ashland Stock Book. *UK*

After several days in Lexington, the Russell family returned by stagecoach to their home in Missouri. Josephine's first visit to Ashland would have a special meaning in the future. She would spend most of her adult life living and working on the Ashland estate and marry two of the men she met, a grandson and a son of Henry Clay.

When the Russell family reached Missouri, the presidential campaign of 1844 was already in progress. In December 1843, Colonel Russell received a letter from his brother Thomas encouraging him to support Henry Clay in the election.

Ash Hill
Dec. 17th 1843

Col. William H. Russell
Fulton, Callaway County, Missouri

My Dear Brother

Well what will interest you the most? As the Yankee says, I will guess the present prospects and future success of old Prince Hal—to whom you are more devoted than many a man to his wife. And indeed I cannot say that your friendship or confidence in him is in the least misplaced—for I am sure he entertains the same kind of friendship for you that you entertain for him. He writes to you, but he spoke to me more explicitly than he ever commits to writing—he is your warm & devoted friend. On Thursday last he left us for New Orleans not to return until after the Baltimore Convention. He will remain some short time in Orleans—pass on to Mobile thence through Alabama, Georgia south and North Carolina on to Virginia & perhaps Maryland—but will be in striking distance of Baltimore at the time of the Convention to make a response if necessary.

The last time I was in Lexington some days ago before he left, we spent one hour or more in the back room of his office—he had that morning received some letters from New York and other Eastern States (which he read to me)—highly satisfactory as to his prospects in 1844. We talked about a variety of matters & things in which he unbosomed himself to me as he would do to a brother or son. And indeed when we parted, I could not but feel considerably affected. He clasped me by the hand & invoked the blessing of God upon me. We may never meet again on earth—he has a long journey before him, but I doubt not he is a Christian, notwithstanding he has never made a public profession. I have promised with my family to visit his [family] during his absence which I will do as soon as our roads become passable. He is a noble old fellow, go ahead for him in Missouri . . . . .

Sarah & the children join me in sending love to you, sister Zanette,[31] the children & all friends.

T. A. Russell[32]

During the following year, Colonel Russell campaigned for Henry Clay and the Whig Party, representing Missouri at the Whig convention that nominated Clay as its candidate for president for the third time. But in November 1844, Clay was again defeated both in Missouri and nationally. The Democratic party candidate, James K. Polk, won the election following an aggressive campaign. His popular position favoring the annexation of Texas and California from Mexico dominated the campaign, while Clay spent too much time responding to old charges of a "corrupt bargain" in connection with the presidential election of 1824. Josephine Clay, who idealized Clay, later wrote:

The personal magnetism of Henry Clay was marvelous. At his defeat in 1844 for the Presidency, a profound sigh seemed wrung from the heart of the nation. Tender women and strong men wept and sorrowed, not as they would have sorrowed over the non-success of merely a political favorite, but for the defeat of one they dearly loved; for the irreparable misfortune which had befallen the United States.[33]

Chapter 2

Travels to California and Mexico

Why doomed ever-lacking the nest
Outward borne with tireless wing?[1]

Colonel Russell made a year-long commitment to the presidential campaign, and after Clay's defeat, he was without any means of supporting his family. He was under pressure to repay a loan he had incurred to purchase a 600 acre farm near Fulton. Russell had given a bond to the former owner, William Breadwell, and the outstanding obligation on March 23, 1846 totaled $2,150. Breadwell demanded repayment and stated to the County Circuit Court that the farm was worth at least $10,000 which Russell disputed. It is not known whether the property was sold at that time or the repayment schedule revised, but it is clear that the Russell family was in need of funds.[2]

Although his brother urged him to return to Kentucky, he wanted to investigate the developing territory of California. He planned to travel alone and would send for his family to join him if he could find employment. In May 1846, he equipped himself with a wagon and several oxen and joined a large party of émigrés in Independence, Missouri. At that time it was the largest wagon train to travel to California—63 wagons, 119 men, 59 women, 110 children, over 700 cattle, and 150 horses. His trip was documented in a daily journal kept by a traveling companion, Edwin Bryant, a newspaper editor from Louisville, Kentucky.[3] Colonel Russell became a popular member of the company, known for public speaking and story telling, and was elected Captain.

In a Pulitzer Prize-winning book about the period, *1846: The Year of Decision* by Bernard DeVoto, Russell was described as "a tall man in a Panama hat, courteous to all around him, a mighty orator and therefore a predestined captain. He got the train in motion somehow; but it was too big and had a fundamental conflict between those going to California and those heading for Oregon."[4]

One story followed Russell to California. It seems that one night in camp after several rounds of home-made liquor, an owl was heard in the distance calling out "Whotu, Whotu." Russell believed he heard a voice calling to him "Who are you?" He called out in a loud voice "Colonel William H. Russell of Kentucky, a bosom friend of Henry Clay." Thereafter, he was known as Owl Russell, a name that followed him to California.[5]

After a few days on the trip, Russell became ill and seemed to get worse as the journey progressed. The route was up the north fork of the Platte River to the Sweetwater River, down the Big Sandy River and the Green River Valley to Fort Bridger (Wyoming), where a trading post had been built by the American Fur Company. Bryant described Fort Bridger "as two or three miserable log cab-

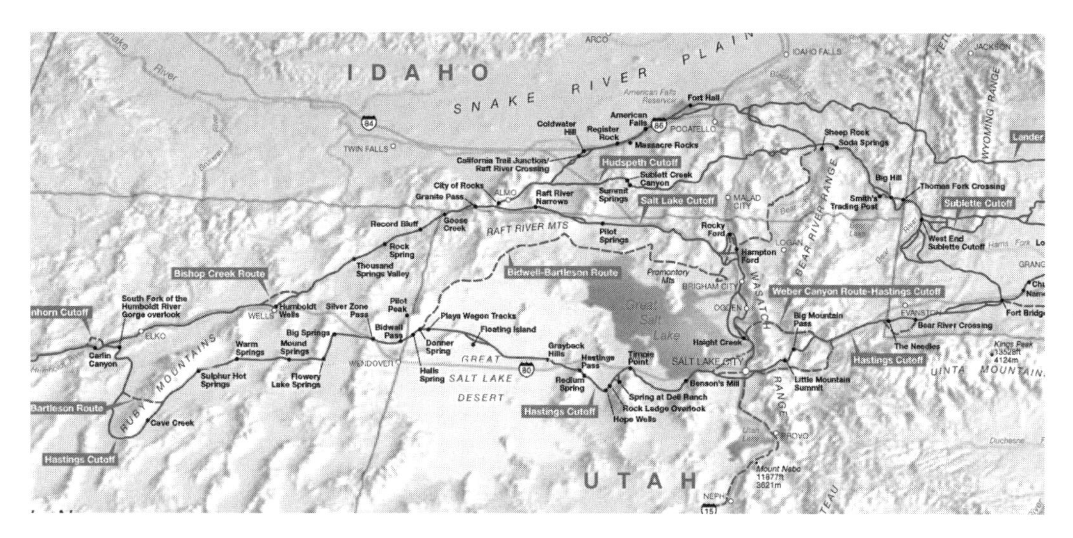

Fig. 2.1 Map of California Trail and the Hastings Cutoff. *National Park Service*

ins, rudely constructed and bearing but a faint resemblance to habitable houses."[6] Here, Colonel Russell began a series of letters to his brother that continued throughout his trip to California. Thomas Russell died on July 6, 1846, but Colonel Russell did not learn about his brother's death until eighteen months later when he returned to Missouri.

When Russell stopped at Fort Bridger to rest the caravan's animals, he was "surrounded by the bustle of mountain men [fur traders] and thousands of Snake Indians." He wrote:

> I have seated myself on the ground and on my knee I will try to scribble something in the shape of a letter. . . . I continued the command of the company until I had nearly reached Fort Larima [Laramie] on the north fork of the Platte, 700 miles west of Independence. Here my health became bad (chills and fever) . . . and I resigned my office in opposition to the wishes of every man and woman in the caravan. I swapped my oxen for mules and packs and with Bryant, young [Richard Taylor] Jacobs of Louisville, Buchanan, William Brown and four others, we are trudging on through the wildest and most savage country that certainly any white man ever went through. It is thought by some dangerous but I consider it safer with nine good and true men than with 100 . . . . Mr. Hastings met us to pilot a new route across the California Mountains. He is a very intelligent man but I think rather ambitious . . . ."[7]

Russell's party had met Lansford W. Hastings, the author of a guide book for traveling west based upon his trips to California and Oregon. He was returning with James M. Hudspeth, after exploring a shortcut around the south end of the Great Salt Lake that would save two hundred miles. Hastings recommended a new route, which required crossing the Wasatch Mountains, a section of the southern shore of the Great Salt Lake, and the Great Salt Lake Desert. But finding the trail very steep and rough in the Wasatch Mountains, Bryant sent letters back to the main party urging travelers with families to take the old trail through Fort Hall north of the Great Salt Lake. The letters were never received.[8]

Two well-to-do brothers, George and Jacob Donner, their relatives, and a large tribe of children were going to California with Russell's caravan to retire to a warmer climate. They fell well behind the main party of travelers and left Fort Bridger eleven days after Russell and Bryant. Hastings agreed to lead the Donner party through the Wasatch Range, but they found it far more difficult than expected. To follow the Hastings Cutoff with pack animals was challenging, but with wagons it was nearly impossible. Boulders had to be removed and a windlass used to pull wagons up the face of cliffs. They required several weeks longer than Bryant and Russell to cross the Wasatch Mountains.

When the Donner party finally passed the south shore of the Great Salt Lake and entered the desert, their supplies of fresh water ran out, and they had to abandon many of their animals. When they emerged from the desert, the men returned with new animals and supplies to rescue wagons left behind. It was October before the Donner party reached the Sierra Nevada Mountains at Truckee Pass, and they met heavy snows. At the summit of the mountains, the snows were five feet deep. Despite several attempts, rescue parties did not reach them until the spring. Of the eighty-one people in the Donner party, forty-five survived the winter. Their story, which included details of eating pack animals and cannibalism, was national news and was told and retold to potential Gold Rush travelers. Perhaps unfairly, Russell was blamed in some accounts of the trip for the decision to abandon the Donner party and travel ahead. The Donner party experience was described as the worst disaster on the trail to California.[9]

After Colonel Russell left for California, Zaenett wrote to her brother-in-law Thomas that she was short of funds and could not continue the private tutor for her children. Her three older boys, Robert, Egbert and Frederick, had finished their schooling, but Thomas, Henry Clay, Josephine, and George Washington would have to continue their home education alone.

8th June 1846

Col. Thomas A. Russell
Lexington, Kentucky

Dear Brother

I should have written to you immediately on my return home but was prevented by indisposition from which I have not yet entirely recovered. I endeavored to see you again before you left Independence and feel almost ashamed to acknowledge the true Cause, the want of fortitude. I endeavored to avoid every thing that might disqualify me for the severe trial that was soon to take place .... I remained nearly two weeks after you left, rode out to the encampment about fifteen miles from Independence ...a finer looking company never left our borders; I became well acquainted with those noble young men from your state all of whom Kentucky may well be proud of. It is needless to say how I parted with my husband, enough it is past and I am here struggling with life's many ills . . .my children all of them endeavor to lighten my affliction and make tolerable my solitary situation; and if I had the means of educating them I should be comparatively happy with your kind assistance and the hire of servants we have left.

I am [farming] to pay off the small claims that are against us and hope by the time that my husband returns they will all be satisfied; which I know will be very gratifying to him with the pleasure of seeing him restored to his former peace and tranquility . . . I regret excessively being compelled to keep Jose [Josephine] at home, it will be a serious loss to her and nothing is so horrible to me as the idea of raising my children in ignorance. I would do anything on earth to prevent it.

I received a letter from Wm Russell at Kansas River hundred and twenty miles from Independence, it was the last opportunity he would have of writing and I imagine he wrote to you from the same place. He was elected Capt. by a large majority four out of five and was getting on finely. I know his spirits are miserable and nothing but his pride sustains him.

Sincerely yours, Z. Russell[8]

Zaenett was determined that Josephine should receive a good education and encouraged her to read books of literature brought to Missouri by her mother's family when they visited from Maryland. Josephine responded enthusiastically, but her brothers considered her eccentric because she spent long hours reading. They called her a "bluestocking," a derogatory term used at the time to refer to girls that were more focused on academic studies than household duties. Undeterred, she began to think of a career in writing.[9]

When Colonel Russell reached the west coast in the fall 1846 and settled in the small community of Yerba Buena (San Francisco) with only a few hundred people, situated on the south side of a large bay about six miles from the Pacific Ocean. He quickly became acquainted with other travelers in the area from Kentucky and Missouri.

In the early evening of October 3, Commodore Robert Stockton of the U. S. Navy arrived by sailing vessel to serve as commander-in-chief of the Americans who claimed the territory of California. Russell was asked to chair the Commodore's reception and serve as orator of the day. His speech welcomed the Commodore as he landed from his barge at the docks where Clay Street is now located.[10] "His speech was bombastic, in spread-eagle style saying 'I meet and welcome you on the shore'—giving much emphasis to the consonants."[11]

Commodore Stockton called for volunteers to fight the Mexican administration. By the time he left San Francisco, he had a force of 428 men, including experienced American riflemen and a party of Walla-Walla Indians from Oregon. U. S. Army Colonel John C. Frémont, a topographical engineer, was placed in charge, and he chose Russell as ordnance officer.[12]

The volunteers called themselves the "California Battalion" and began marching south toward Los Angeles while U. S. Army General Stephen W. Kearny with a force of ninety veterans of the Mexican War moved north from New Mexico toward Los Angeles. In early December 1846 Frémont reached San Luis Obispo, a stronghold of the Mexicans and took it by surprise without firing a gun, capturing the commandant, Don Jesus Pico. On December 16, 1846, a court martial was convened for Don Jesus, who had been captured previously and released after agreeing to support the Americans. He was charged with breaking parole and sentenced to be hanged. A group of Mexican ladies met with Russell and asked for a reprieve. After listening to their pleas, Russell intervened with Colonel Frémont, who issued a pardon. A grateful Mexican lady gave Russell a colorful scarf which he later gave to his daughter Josephine.[13] Don Jesus was a cousin of Don Andreas Pico, the commander of the Mexican forces, and he assisted Russell in negotiations to end the conflict.[14]

On January 10, Kearny and Stockton entered Los Angeles unopposed; the Mexican forces had moved northward. Frémont's troops camped first in Santa Barbara and then moved south toward San Fernando. On January 13, Mexican peace-commissioners appeared near their camp at Couenga Ranch on the San Gabriel River and agreed to surrender.[15]

The terms of capitulation to the United States, negotiated by Frémont and Russell, acknowledged U. S. control of the territory of California but required no oath of loyalty and extended amnesty to the Mexicans. It was strongly opposed by General Kearny, who believed that he should dictate the terms of the agreement as President Polk's representative. Over General Kearny's objections, Commodore Stockton appointed Frémont acting governor of the new Territory of California and Russell secretary of state. There followed a period of conflict between the senior officers of the U.S. Army and Navy over civil control of California. Kearny demanded that Frémont, who was acting under the authority of Commodore Stockton, acknowledge Kearny's authority as his superior Army officer. When he refused, Kearny moved his headquarters to Monterey, established a civil government, and declared Frémont and Russell to be deposed. General Kearny ordered a court martial for Colonel Frémont on charges of disobeying a superior officer and mutiny. Frémont began a series of appeals to his father-in-law, Senator Thomas Hart Benton of Missouri, to restore his authority.[16]

Henry Clay's correspondence with Zaenett Russell indicated that he favored the restoration of Frémont and Russell to their positions.

> Mrs. Russell,
>
> I received your letter and the one accompanying it from Col. Russell. I have frequently received letters from him during his absence, and from them had learnt the difficulties arising out of the collision between the American Commanders for the Government in California. Believing that Gov. Fremont and Col. Russell ought to be sustained in authority, before the receipt of your letter, I had written to that effect to a friend [John J. Crittenden] in the Senate. And I shall take great pleasure, and be most happy, to do anything in my power (altho' I fear that will not be much) to uphold their power and authority. I dare say, however, that they will have more efficient friends than I am, altho' more faithful and anxious they could not have . . . .H. Clay[17]

Frémont asked Russell to support his cause and to testify on his behalf. Russell agreed to return to Washington, D. C. and had an adventurous crossing, leading a wagon train on the Santa Fe Trail that was attacked three times by Indian raiders.[18] Colonel Russell visited his family in Missouri and his brother, Thomas' family in Lexington before reaching Washington.

On November 2, 1847, the U. S. Army court martial convened at the Washington Arsenal, a huge wooden building. A large crowd of spectators favored Frémont, but the jury of twelve senior army officers viewed him as an army officer who had chosen to obey a rival naval officer. The defense, led by Senator Benton, tried to dramatize in the press that Frémont, a brave hero who gained California for the U. S., was martyred by incompetents in the army. Russell was among the witnesses supporting Frémont.[19]

On January 17, 1848, the tension of the trial was broken temporarily by the wedding of Senator Benton's daughter, Sarah, to Richard Taylor Jacob, the Kentuckian who traveled to California with Russell and Bryant and served in the California Battalion. He was in Washington as a defense witness.[20] President Polk did not attend the wedding as expected, but the opposition leader Henry Clay, whose son James was married to Jacob's sister Susan, escorted the couple to their wedding table. Colonel Russell was probably one of the celebrants.

On January 29, the trial of Frémont was over and the verdict announced. The army officers on the jury could not accept the disobedience of an officer to his superior, and Frémont was convicted on all counts. However, the jury recommended leniency. President Polk, who had remained silent, was under strong political pressure from Congress, and he dismissed the charge of mutiny, remitted the sentence for Frémont, and restored him to service in the army. Frémont, however, resigned from the service shortly thereafter.[21]

In the spring 1848, Colonel Russell participated in another attempt to nominate Clay as the Whig Party candidate for president. The Kentuckian was defeated for the nomination, and Russell left the convention before the final vote, cursing the supporters of "Old Rough and Ready" Gen. Zachary Taylor, who was nominated and then elected president.[22]

Russell hoped for a government appointment in California, but his actions at the Whig Convention and involvement in the Frémont trial again exposed him to criticism. In spring 1849, he was invited to participate as an honorary member of the California Constitutional Convention. Josephine was now thirteen and bored with her home studies. Colonel Russell and Zaenett wanted Josephine to learn more about the country by accompanying her father on the trip west. Zaenett and the two younger boys, Henry Clay, twelve, and George Washington, ten, would follow if Colonel Russell could obtain a government appointment or develop a law practice that would support their move to California.

The California Gold Rush was in progress, and an estimated 100,000 people migrated to California in 1849. Approximately half came by ship from the east coast using a new steamship service from New York to Panama connecting with overland links across the isthmus to steamships that sailed to California. Most travelers from Missouri went overland on the California Trail by wagon train. But the crowds led many overland travelers to become sick from contaminated water facilities; and for the first time, there was a cholera epidemic on the California Trail.[23]

Russell selected a well organized caravan, and given his experience on the California Trail, probably carried water on the trip. His wagon joined many others assembled on the grasslands at Fitzhugh Mills near Independence, Missouri.

> The campgrounds were always crowded with pioneer homesteaders waiting in readiness for the "roll out" call of the wagon master. There were so many drivers yelling "Whoa! Haw! Goddam ye!" at their oxen that the innocent Indians began to call white men "Goddams" and greeted them with "Whoa-Haw!" in place of "How!"[24]

The caravan left on April 24, 1849.[25] On the trail each night, the wagons were circled and fires were left burning to ward off Indians interested in stealing goods. Josephine and her father often entertained their companions around the campfire by singing and playing the banjo. After the travelers went to sleep on an especially dark night, an Indian crawled into the camp and threw a rope around Josephine's banjo and tried to pull it out of her tent into the shadows. She suddenly awoke and saw the rope, which she grabbed and pulled as hard as she could. The Indian ran but his leather medicine pouch fell to the ground and became a souvenir of the trip.[26]

When they reached California, Colonel Russell and Josephine found a temporary home in San Francisco, and the Colonel began to investigate the opportunities for a legal practice. He completed arrangements for a new law firm in partnership with Edward D. Baker, former U. S. Representative from Illinois and friend of Abraham Lincoln. Colonel Russell was to have an office in San Jose, slated to be the capital of the new state of California, while Baker would represent the firm in San Francisco.[27]

In the fall 1849, Colonel Russell planned to attend the California Constitutional Convention in Monterey, a community of just over one thousand and the capital of the Mexican province of Alta California.[28] Located south of San Francisco on a beautiful peninsula, Monterey had been a larger town than San Francisco until its population was reduced by men leaving for the gold rush.

Fig. 2.2 Indian Medicine Bag Owned by Josephine Russell

Tall sailing ships and steamships regularly stopped at Monterey, the shipping port for produce from the ranches of the central coast valleys and for the import of supplies for the booming gold mines in the mountainous area of Las Mariposas ("butterflies") near Yosemite Valley.[29]

Josephine Russell wrote a letter to a friend or family member describing her impressions of Monterey:

> The approach by water can scarcely be excelled anywhere for beauty of scenery. The bay, a beautiful skirt of water, which curves gracefully, and on our side without a single indentation rolls back to the broad ocean. Far back on green hills in all their gloomy majesty, the dark majestic pines and oaks cast their shadow on the myriads of lovely wildflowers. I say there is romance enough to get a poet crazy and even to kindle a spark of sentiment in the bosom of an incorrigible old bachelor. I freely confess that I always feel particularly amiable towards all mankind after a sylvan ramble through nature's green bowers but to descend to the commonalities of life.
>
> The houses are principally old fashion Mexican adobe buildings constructed very evidently with a much greater reference to comfort, strictly speaking, than appearance. These are placid and generally walled-in where the owners happened to have a piece of ground. This irregularity does not look as badly as you might suppose. It gives the City an independent, don't care look which I admire. This place used to be the capital and quite flourishing, but gold has visited many of its citizens so that now it is about half its normal size and almost totally bereft of business. The Spanish towns are all a facsimile of each other. Those of any energy in business habits are trying their luck among the Yankees. In some portions of Cal, the climate is variable and intense in its extremes as in your own native state. Generally the climate [in Monterey] is good and would compare well with the brightest sunshine of Italy.[30]

Colonel Russell rented an adobe house near the residence of an artist who served as the mayor of Monterey.[31] John C. Frémont and his wife Jesse Benton Frémont also arrived in Monterey for the California Constitutional Convention and rented a house near the sea.

When the convention began, most of the delegates favored immediate statehood for California. After six weeks of debate, a constitution was drafted based upon the new state of Iowa. The most important dispute concerned the eastern boundary of the state; delegates finally agreed on a line in the Sierra Nevada Mountains. The U. S. Congress was divided about the slavery issue in California, but a compromise originated by Henry Clay and steered through the Congress by Stephen A. Douglas of Illinois, gave the authority to each western territory to settle its own position on slavery. The California Convention decided against slavery. The California statehood bill was signed on October 13, 1849.[32]

Henry Clay took an active role in helping Colonel Russell obtain a government appointment in California. Clay wrote a letter to President Zachary Taylor's representative expressing his disappointment that Russell had not been named "to an Indian Agency in that State." John J. Crittenden, the U. S. attorney general and former senator from Kentucky, had vetoed his appointment, complaining that Colonel Russell had used "passionate expressions towards him in reference to the nomination of General Taylor." Clay responded that a Mr. Barbour was appointed, "who I am informed, used quite as exceptionable language toward me, as any Col. Russell could have employed . . . ." But Clay insisted, "for this I do not care a straw." Clay declared that Russell was "one of the Pioneers to California," who "had much intercourse with the Civilized Indians in that State, brought several back to Missouri, one of whom remained with me several months," and praised his "prominent part in the Whig party" of Missouri. On behalf of this "interprizing (sic), brave, intelligent and honorable" man who had been "a most zealous & faithful friend," Clay took "the liberty to ask the President to reconsider the case of Col. Russell."[33] After President Taylor died suddenly of food poisoning, his successor Millard

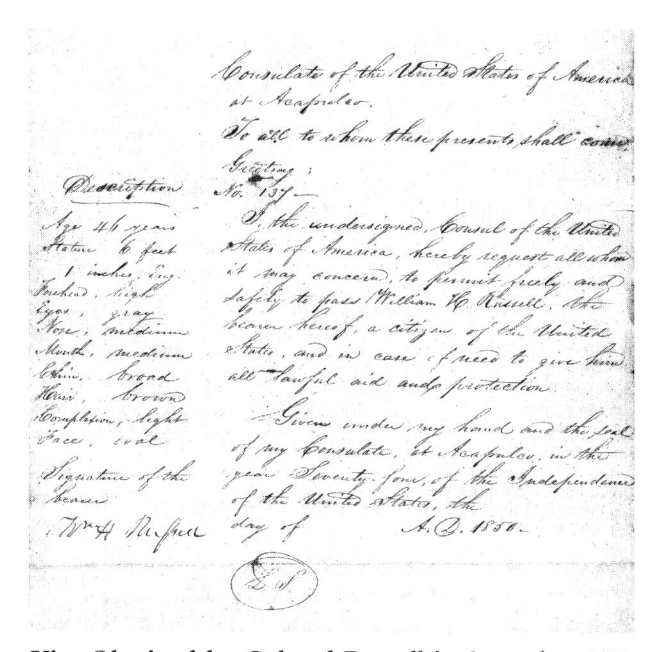
Consulate of the United States of America
at Acapulco.
To all to whom these presents shall come,
Greeting;
No. 137—

Description
Age 46 years
Stature 6 feet
1 inches, Eng.
Forehead, high
Eyes, gray
Nose, medium
Mouth, medium
Chin, broad
Hair, brown
Complexion, light
Face, oval

Signature of the
bearer
Wm H Russell

I, the undersigned, Consul of the United States of America, hereby request all whom it may concern, to permit freely and safely to pass William H. Russell, the bearer hereof, a citizen of the United States, and in case of need to give him all lawful aid and protection.

Given under my hand and the seal of my Consulate, at Acapulco, in the year Seventy-four, of the Independence of the United States, the day of A.D. 1850.

L.S.

Fig. 2.3 Mexican Visa Obtained by Colonel Russell in Acapulco. *UK*

Fillmore appointed Russell Collector of U. S. Customs in Monterey on March 7, 1851.[34]

Josephine Clay's novel *Uncle Phil* tells a story very similar to her own family experience.

> Many years previous [the colonel's] large estate had been swallowed up by the too ardent support of a political friend who failed in his election. Finding himself in the position of

> a financially ruined man he willingly accepted the office. . . . in a far away place. . . the genial, popular gentleman was appointed collector of customs.[35]

With the conclusion of the Mexican War, Colonel Russell wanted to do legal work to support trade between Mexico and California. An American friend in Mexico City, Mr. Hargous, agreed to work with Colonel Russell's clients. In 1850, Russell obtained a passport from the U. S. Consulate in Acapulco and visited Mexico. In May 1851, he again visited Mexico and this time took Josephine with him.

Father and daughter traveled on the steamship *Alabama* to Acapulco with family friends. Josephine saved a poem written by a friend in their traveling party.[36]

> To Miss Josephine.
>
> Many rays are on thy fair brow,
> In bright effluence cast around,
> May calm; and gentle thought, as now
> And sweet content thy life surround.
> May God above, his grace impart
> To thee. Lead, protect and bless,
> May true exalted glory thee begivt (sic),
> Recurring peace and happiness,
> Thus wisdom's unfailing wreath will thee
> That adorns, create the heart divine.
>
> Alabama at Sea
>
> Latitude 20.50, Longitude 95.42 West [The ship was located north of Acapulco just off the coast of Mexico]
>
> May 11th 1851. Robt. W. Foster[37]

The trip from Acapulco to Mexico City was by wagon and mule over rutted tracks through a series of towns in the mountains surrounding Mexico City. The roads were very poor. The country they passed was barren basaltic rock with little water in the landscape.[38]

Arriving at Mexico City, Josephine described what she saw:

> A wonderful transformation was wrought in the fair landscape in the vicinity of the old city of Teuschititlan, the metropolis of the Aztec empire—now called Mexico City—midway between the Atlantic and the Pacific and on the summit of the Cordilleras, and secluded from the outer world by a mountain barrier. Southward and eastward, rising in their eternal glory, are the ever snow-crowned Popacatepetl and Iztaccihuatl—the "White Lady."[39]

Mexico City contained a series of large squares with fountains in the center of each. The Spanish section had houses built of stone with flat roofs and courtyards with Moorish tile decoration. The native Indians lived in mud houses.[40]

Mr. Hargous' wife Susan arranged for Josephine to meet a group of young people in Mexico City, and she was introduced to a young captain of the Mexican army, Francisco Ramiro. He was much taken with her. When Josephine complained about having to eat with the copper utensils she was carrying on the trip, Ramiro presented her with a heavy Mexican silver spoon engraved with "Miss Russell from Francisco Ramiro, Mexico, June 1851."

Fig. 2.4 Mexican Silver Spoon Presented to Josephine Russell in Mexico, June 1851

Josephine did not see him again, but she later learned of his role in an incident in Mexico. She read in a newspaper in 1867 that Ramiro was part of a force commanded by the Mexican leader Benito Pablo Juarez that overthrew the French-sponsored government of Mexico, and Captain Ramiro signed Emperor Maximilian's death warrant before he was shot.[41]

After Josephine and her father returned to Monterey, Susan Hargous wrote a letter to Josephine:

> Mexico, Aug 13th 1851
>
> My Dear Josephine
>
> I am indeed sorry to hear you had such a very unpleasant voyage. I hope long before this, you are quite recovered, and also your Father. We heard from you at Acapulco through Mr. Foster, who reported all [is] well & a very sudden departure, which I thought quite fortunate for you, as I have an idea that Acapulco is very dull & uninteresting.
>
> I can scarcely give you any news of your traveling companions, as I have not seen them since you left & what I have heard of them, I would not like to commit to paper . . . .
>
> Have you heard from your Mother, and when will she go out? You had not been in Monterey long enough to know if you liked it or not; write to me soon; tell me if you have commenced Spanish & how you like your new home. I hope you may like it very much for I think there is nothing so dreadful as homesickness, a feeling that I suffer with whenever I receive a letter from home and whenever Mr. H. is sick. Miss Wight sends her best love to you both, and joins us in hoping that your health is quite restored, and also that of your Father, that you may find Monterey an agreeable residence & that we may sooner or later be able to do ourselves the pleasure of accepting your Father's kind invitation of visiting you at Monterey . . . .
>
> Hoping to hear from you soon, I remain as ever yours, etc.
>
> Susan J. Hargous[42]

A California newspaper requested that Colonel Russell keep a journal of his trip to Mexico, and he assigned the task to Josephine. When they returned, it was reported that she prepared an article for the California newspapers that ended with "my father made me do this."[43]

Chapter 3

Romance in Monterey

T'was joy, only joy that reigned supreme
And life fair as an enchanted dream . . . .[1]

Shortly after Colonel Russell and Josephine returned from Mexico during the summer of 1851, they were joined by other members of Russell family. Josephine's mother and younger brothers arrived in Monterey after an overland wagon trip from Missouri. The family continued to rent a house in Monterey and was provided with an apartment in the customs house as well.

The original stone customs house dating from 1823 contained two-story wings and verandas on the east and north sides. It was rebuilt in 1841 with an eighty-foot room in the center used to inspect goods. This room also served as a ballroom during frequent Mexican-American festivals held in the community. The customs house stood opposite a wharf from which goods were received from ships.[2] The calling cards in Josephine's scrapbook include the names of prominent Californians and visitors from the East. Colonel Russell and his friend Edwin Bryant had visited the ranch of the early Swiss-German settler, Johann August Sutter when they first arrived in California. Sutter visited the Colonel in Monterey after he became a victim of the gold rush. In 1841 he had been granted a vast tract of land in the Sacramento Valley by the Mexican governor of California to establish the new kingdom of "Neuve Helvetio." After becoming the richest and most respected citizen of California, he lost all of his property when thousands of prospectors overran his land and became squatters. Colonel Russell had written a letter on behalf of Sutter to the U.S. Court arguing that Sutter should retain possession of his property.[3]

Samuel Colt was also a guest. Colt owned a factory in Connecticut that produced repeating pistols for the U. S. forces fighting in the Mexican War and was seeking to sell his weapons to the new government of California. While visiting, he taught Josephine to shoot his pistol. When Colt left to return to the east, he gave Josephine one of his pistols, and she developed a habit of riding horseback in the nearby mountains with the pistol in her belt.[4]

Among the calling cards in Josephine's scrapbook are several cards from Douglas Ottinger, captain of the U. S. Revenue Cutter, *Frolic.* Captain Ottinger worked closely with Colonel Russell to enforce customs regulations and became a hero to the Colonel and his daughter.

Ships from many nations were avoiding Monterey due to the actions of sailor thieves. Merchants had a practice of hiring the crew for their clipper ships at local boarding houses at a rate of thirty to forty dollars a month, two months-wages being paid in advance. On the night before the ship was scheduled to sail, thieves would come on board each ship and take the crew back to the shore and

Fig. 3.1 The Old Customs House in Monterey. *California State Parks*

deliver them to a new boarding house where they would again sign up for service on a waiting ship and receive advance wages.[5]

Captain Ottinger established a "mayday" signal with the master of each merchant ship. If a ship hoisted the colors in a certain manner during the day, or at night placed two lanterns about six feet apart one above the other, the well armed *Frolic* would come to the rescue. Upon boarding the threatened ship, Captain Ottinger would order the crew to quarters and provide small arms to the officers on the ship and prepare for a fight. The *Frolic* stood ready to fire its guns at any pirate ship that tried to intervene. His methods were so successful that the thieves openly threatened to board and destroy the *Frolic*, but the threat was never carried out.[6]

In her autobiographical novel *Uncle Phil*, Josephine describes meeting an older friend of her father, who may be modeled after Captain Ottinger. Using thinly disguised characters, she identified with Geraldine Southampton, a young lady from Virginia, and modeled a character after her father, Colonel Southampton, the collector of customs in the fictional town of Bonito. Paul Smith is her father's friend.

> She sped to the office apartment now closed, office hours being over. The room was not attractive, desks and stools its only furniture, but the young lady was never happier in her life. The idea that she was about to transact business was positively bewitching.
>
> She seated herself quickly, pulling up to her the huge Government inkstand with its bristling array of pens. Then the form book was opened, and . . . she promptly decided to do the work. At her back was an open window, through which streamed the sun's rays—silent, potent rays, laded with odylic fluid—passing back and forth, over and around her—noiseless, invisible, mysterious forces, actively weaving their wondrous tissues and indissolubly uniting her life with that of another life, standing in the doorway.
>
> A man, certainly older than her father, had entered the room. His rugged features were grave even to sternness. Not a person to incommode, was written in legible characters

from head to foot. The self-confidence of his bearing denoted a man who was all and all to his own requirements.

The deference usual in accosting strangers of the opposite sex was out of the experience of Miss Southampton. Men of every age and degree had gone down before her without the least hesitation, without the slightest protest. But there was something disconcerting in this newcomer's steady gaze; yet never was a Southampton born to blanch and she demanded, authoritatively: "Did you not see that the flag was down, and that office hours were over?"

And why she refrained from telling him that he was disturbing her, and request his absence, was the perplexing question. She was under the spell of some strange, new, compelling influence, and chafed under it. . . . With heightened color, and without a word, she recommenced her writing; but the usually facile pen became an awkward stick—it was impossible to write with that glum man looking on, and he must be got rid of. . . .

"You might smoke a cigar in the corridor while waiting."

"I do not care to smoke, and will wait where I am," he answered with decision. . . .

With her quick ears, she caught the sound of her father's footsteps. In a moment more, he had entered the room.

With exclamation of delight the two men clasped hands. . . . In the warmth of their greeting it was some moments before the Colonel recollected to say: "Ah, here is my little daughter."

Why is it, no matter how well-grown a girl may be, she is invariably introduced by her father after this fashion? The introduction was acknowledged by the lady with cold dignity; by the gentleman without enthusiasm.

"You have a name, I suppose?"

"My name is Smith," responded the gentleman. My Christian name is Paul—if you have any interest in knowing," showing some annoyance.

But the Colonel, observing with concern that his daughter and his guest were not taking to each other, hastened to interpose.

"Come," said he, "let's get into more comfortable quarters."

"As for myself, I have that clearance to finish," said Miss Southamption, with gravity.

"Never mind the clearance, one of the clerks will finish it. I want you with us." So together they proceeded to that part of the building where there were apartments fitted up for the family.

It was a cosy parlor into which they entered. The lace curtains and the upright piano had been brought from Paris, the comfortable bamboo chairs from Boston, and the knick-knacks from Japan and various parts of the globe—all uniting to form that refinement of luxury with which those who have pride in pluralizing their ancestors take pains to surround themselves.

The door was left wide open to enjoy a view of the beautiful bay; the tide rushing in with a gentle purr almost lapped the foundations of the wooden corridor. Sometimes the heavy billows from the offing thundered in with a tumultuous dash, when the doors had to be closed to keep out the drenching spray.

"And now, Gerry, a party of us are going to the Point.[7] I have promised a mussel stew, and won't you go along to make it pleasant for us?"

"Papa," she answered, solemnly, "I am never going to another mussel stew. . . ."

"Oh! yes you will, Gerry," said he, coaxingly. Miss Southampton finally comes to terms. Later on, when she made her appearance at the designated place, where the mussels congregate, it was quite evident that the joyous spirit, which had seemed part of her, was still under a cloud.

Mr. Smith has seen a good deal of the world, and had no difficulty in making up his mind that his old friend's daughter is the worst case of "spoiled" that ever came under his observation. But [he also thought] "not a particularly bad sort, wonderfully handsome . . . ."[8]

In March 1851, Colonel Russell invited Captain Ottinger to spend a weekend with his family in Monterey. The forty-eight-year-old married man was fascinated with Josephine's lively conversation. They attended a Mexican fiesta in the great room at the customs house and a "metaphysical" play that Captain Ottinger said he did not understand.

When he wrote to Josephine after the weekend, it was apparent that they had a special relationship.

Onboard U. S. Cutter "Frolic"
San Francisco March 27

My Dear Joe

I saw Mary & Lu [Moore] last evening [in San Francisco] and we all agree in the fact that you are a lovable little girl, it was exceedingly difficult for me to keep the triangle with equal sides—for I found one of them inclined to elongate—almost irresistibly. But I must not love Jose more than I do Ginny [his daughter] and I think of Jose now as often as I do of her. I have some matters of public interest to settle with your father and must make that an excuse for visiting Monterey soon.

Do you know Joe that I am made better by my association with your family. I am sensible of its influence upon me, and much gratified in feeling the good effect. I do not believe that I should have offered the priest a passage, or have waited for him, had it not been that Jose was of his church. Yet I am doubly paid for that act not only in thinking it might please you but in making an agreeable acquaintance also. . . . . I am conjuring on the probabilities of you and your Mother becoming acquainted with Mrs. Ottinger & Ginny, I am sure [you] would love them . . . . I regret that your Father had not been born a prince—Oh! No—for then I should not have known you, so that it is all just right as it is . . . .

Yours, D. O.[9]

Their personal correspondence continued for eighteen months. Several of the letters from Captain Ottinger to Josephine are very personal. Her letters have been lost, but it is apparent that she reciprocated. The captain was assigned duties in San Francisco, but he visited Monterey on several occasions to see Josephine. Josephine's friend Mary Moore who lived in San Francisco wrote to her frequently:

Sunday, April 11 [1852]
[San Francisco]

Miss Joe Russell
Customs House
Monterey, Cal.

I add a few lines to the little note which I had intended to have sent by the "Ohio." Your paternal & maternal ancestors arrived here safely this morning bringing us the welcome letters from you. But how "short and sweet" all your letters are. Upon my word! I do think you might write a good long letter. I am sitting in a cold room—sneezing with a rapidity which can hardly be equaled.

All the folks have retired for the night and I suppose that mother little thinks I am writing now. Remember me to Allen & Don Esteoan with many thanks for their letters and a promise to write soon. What a good time you must be having now with the Capitan. Well good-night, do write and use all your influence in making the Capitan do the same. Con muchas expresiones

de amistad
estoy ser Maria[10]
half past ten o'clock

On November 13, 1852 Captain Ottinger wrote that "I attended the wedding of our friend . . . who did not tell me of her intention to make that important change in her life, as you have promised to do. I suppose Mary will soon follow her example, and Jose may be inclined to do the same . . . ."[11]

Uncle Phil introduces another character who falls in love with Geraldine Southampton. Lt. Charley Wood, from a prominent family in Virginia, a neighbor of Colonel Southampton in Virginia, arrives in California and is posted to the local U. S. Army fort. He is treated like a son by Colonel Southampton. This character appears to be modeled after Eugene Erwin, the young grandson of Henry Clay who arrived in Monterey during the summer of 1851.

Colonel Russell was anxious that his daughter marry the grandson of his mentor and Eugene Erwin became a frequent guest at the Russell's home. Before long, Josephine and Eugene were engaged to be married. But she did not forget the adventurous U. S. Coast Guard captain. Her first novel written twenty-two years later was dedicated to "Captain Douglas Ottinger of the U. S. Coast Guard Cutter Frolic."[12]

Eugene Erwin was twenty-one, about five years older than Josephine. A daguerreotype of Eugene in a leather case owned by Josephine shows a good-looking young man in a formal stiff white shirt, with long dark hair. He stares directly at you, conveying an image of strength of character.

Henry Clay was fond of his grandson. After his schooling at the Kentucky Military Institute, Clay took Eugene Erwin to Washington and explored an appointment to West Point. His application was unsuccessful, perhaps due to the fact that another grandson, Henry Clay III, was a cadet

Fig. 3.2 Josephine Deborah Russell **Fig. 3.3 Andrew Eugene Erwin**

at the time with a poor record (he was eventually expelled). Clay arranged a temporary job for Eugene in Washington and then wrote to his contacts to introduce his grandson. Erwin accepted a job in a New York mercantile house but continued to seek a more challenging assignment.[13] On March 7, 1851, Henry Clay wrote that he "has finally determined to go to California in the employment of the Aspinwalls who are engaged in steamship navigation. He will leave [Washington] tomorrow to embark for New Orleans and Chagres [River in Panama] about the last of this month."[14] Eugene Erwin was hired to keep the accounts for the growing business of the Pacific Mail and Steamship Company in Monterey.

Henry Clay and his friends with connections in California wrote letters of introduction for Eugene Erwin. The author of one of the letters would play a role in his future.

Ohio River
18th March 1851

Col. G. Hays

Dear Sir. This will introduce to your further acquaintance Mr. Eugene Erwin, for whom I ask, as an old friend and companion in arms, your special attention. Mr. Erwin is the grandson of Henry Clay, and will no doubt be enthusiastically recommended to the citizens of the land to which he goes a stranger but I wish that you and he should be particularly known to each other.

You will find in times of calm & serenity a desirable friend, and if the storm should burst upon you "he will tie to." Any services you may render him will fall on the kind of man [who] knows how to appreciate & [will be] acknowledged as a personal favor by your friend.

Jefferson Davis[15]

When Eugene arrived in Monterey, he received word that his father, James Erwin, had died in Lexington of complications from an earlier stroke. His father's estate was complex and his assets disputed by creditors. Henry Clay represented Eugene's interests in the estate and informed him about his rights. He wrote to his grandson asking him to appoint a guardian and urged him to live an exemplary life.

Ashland, 19th July 1851

Dear Eugene,

I received your letter of the 30th of May, and I was glad to hear of your safe arrival in good health at San Francisco, and that you were pleased with the country and with your prospects. I was also much gratified to perceive that you had a due sense of the great responsibility of your present condition. You are at a great distance from all your friends. You are very young, and you will be constantly exposed to temptations which if you have not the firmness to resist them may lead to your ruin. Let me entreat you to avoid all dissipations and above all the vice of gambling. It is always attended with loss of character, loss of health, and often the loss of fortune. Those who indulge in it most, and if apparently successful in the hazards of the game, are nevertheless finally losers. Let me also entreat you to avoid all bad company, and to seek the society of those who are respectable, intelligent and upright. This advice is given to you by one who has lived long in the world, and who has had extensive opportunities of witnessing the ruin and desolation produced by dissipated habits and bad company. . . .

Your father left no will, and left his estate in the greatest possible embarrassment. Nobody has administered it, and nobody probably will. Your brother Henry is understood to have some property under his control, but what it is I do not know. Your stepmother and her children remain at Woodlands[107] and I believe are all well. She had an infant son a few days after your father's death. The Woodlands, slaves, and other property will be sold either this fall or next spring. I am paying some attention to your interests and I hope there will be saved to each of you out of the wreck of your father's estate some seven or eight thousand dollars apiece. I think it will be very well for you in your next letter to inform me who you would like to be appointed your guardian during your minority. My age and infirmities are too great for me to act in that character.... Your affectionate grandfather. H. Clay.[17]

Josephine Russell's photograph shows that she had grown to be a very attractive young lady, carefully composed and mature for her age, with dark curly hair and brown eyes. As in the past, no expense was spared in the Russell lifestyle, and Josephine was dressed in the latest fashions of the day.

Colonel Russell strongly encouraged her relationship with Eugene Erwin, and he was hopeful that through his daughter, the Russell family would be more closely associated with the Clay family in the future.

Colonel Russell enthusiastically approved of their engagement and made plans to return east with the couple. Henry Clay did not live to see his grandson's marriage. On June 29, 1852, he died in his room at the National Hotel in Washington, D. C., with his son Thomas at his bedside. He had lost a long battle with tuberculosis at age seventy-five.

In March 1853 Eugene Erwin considered staying in California when he appeared to be in line to receive a government post in the new state. His Aunt Jane, who had married Senator John Bell of Tennessee, arranged through her husband for the new president, Franklin Pierce, to appoint Erwin to a senior position. His appointment was approved by the Pierce Cabinet, but when it was sent to Congress for confirmation, the appointment was blocked by John C. Frémont despite his friendship with the Russell family. He was now a Democratic senator from California and had his own candidate. Eugene's aunt wrote to tell Eugene that the appointment was turned down.[18]

President Pierce removed Colonel Russell from his position as collector of customs in May 1853. As the following letter indicates, the transition was far from smooth.

> To: Col. Wm H. Russell
> Sept. 2nd 1853
>
> My Dear Sir
>
> I transmit herewith a communication from the Comptroller of the Treasury directing you to deliver to me "all the public property in your possession, together with the forms, books of Entry, and instructions relating to the duties of the office with which you a "Collector & Inspector" were furnished by the Department. I will thank you to furnish me with such other books and papers as are in your possession, which properly belong to this office. In the absence of all books and vouchers it is impossible to furnish such information as had been required of me on several occasions, I must beg your early attention to this matter.
>
> Isaac B. Wall, Collector
> Dist of Monterey[19]

The unfortunate Mr. Wall was murdered while serving in office.[20]

Colonel Russell, Josephine, and Eugene began their trip east on "The Accessory Transit Service of Nicaragua," a new transcontinental travel service owned and operated by the shipping magnate Commodore Cornelius Vanderbilt. After failing to gain U. S. government backing for building a canal across the isthmus of Nicaragua, Vanderbilt developed a connecting steamship service between San Francisco and New York with a land crossing in Nicaragua competing with the more established Panama service. In 1851, an advertisement in the *Daily Alta California* newspaper offered:

> "Nicaragua Route! Vanderbilt's Independent Line! Fare Reduced! Through Tickets to New York. For San Juan del Sud. Only twelve miles of land travel thorough a most healthy section of the country, and on the lake steamers . . . in readiness to convey passengers at once to . . . the Atlantic where they will find a new and magnificent steamer for New York direct."[21]

Vanderbilt had been a strong supporter of Henry Clay's campaigns for president in 1844 and 1848, and it is not surprising that the Russell-Erwin party chose to use the Vanderbilt service to return to Kentucky. They received a special introduction to the captain of the steamship from San Francisco to Nicaragua.[22]

Agency, The Accessory Transit Co. of Nicaragua

To Captain J. H. Blethim, S. S. Sierra Nevada — San Francisco, May 16, 1853

Dear Sir: The family of Colonel Russell of Kentucky are passengers on your ship accompanied by Mr. Irwin (sic) grandson of Henry Clay. Please extend to them your kindest attentions during the voyage and do all in your power to make them comfortable.

Very truly yours, E. K. Jamison, Agent[23]

The first leg of the trip was by steamship from San Francisco to a small seaport on the west coast of Nicaragua, San Juan del Sud. No information is available about the Nicaragua crossing of the Russell-Erwin party, but it was probably unpleasant and difficult.

A group of travelers at this time who "felt impelled by a sense of duty to the traveling community" published an article in the *Daily Alta California* which described their experience in Nicaragua. Upon arrival at San Juan del Sud, they found the roads almost impassable with mud two feet deep, and all of the travelers including several ladies were put astride mules in drenching rain and were detained two weeks in the twelve-mile land crossing to Lake Nicaragua, where steamships were to be waiting. They found that the only lake steamer had been damaged in a prior trip when it went over a shallow falls in the connecting river. They stopped for four or five days. Finally they chartered bungays, and made a dangerous trip across the lake in heavy weather during which they were compelled to row all night to the small village of Greytown on the east coast of Nicaragua. When they arrived, their steamer to New York had already sailed.[24]

Five years later, Mark Twain visited Nicaragua on a trip from San Francisco to the east coast and published a series of letters that shocked the public with its descriptions of poor conditions that resulted in long delays and several deaths from cholera.[25]

Mrs. Eugene Erwin

Chapter 4

Erwin Family Life

Soft winds belong to that era most blest,
When springtime harbored not tears.[1]

The announcement of the engagement of Josephine Russell and Eugene Erwin and their subsequent arrival in Lexington was a cause for celebration at Ashland. Although Josephine had visited Lexington several times as a young girl, she was now introduced as a future member of the family and warmly welcomed. A formal dress ball was held at Ashland to honor the couple.[2]

In Lexington, Josephine spent time with Eugene's grandmother, Mrs. Lucretia Clay who told her the story of the life and tragic death of Eugene's mother, Anne Brown Clay. Born in 1807, Anne was the fifth of the eleven children of Henry and Lucretia Clay. She was blessed with an attractive, outgoing personality and was popular with the Clay family. Henry Clay's friends remarked that she was very much like her father.

James Erwin arrived in 1822 from Tennessee to study law at Transylvania College and became acquainted with Anne. He proposed marriage and asked Henry Clay for permission to wed his daughter. He was twenty-seven, and she was sixteen at the time. Henry Clay expressed concern about his lack of knowledge of the Erwin family as well as the age difference. He made it known to James Erwin that he wanted more information before giving his approval, and Erwin arranged for letters of reference to be sent to Henry Clay.[3]

Henry Clay learned that the Erwin family was originally from Virginia, of Scots-Irish ancestry, and that James' father, Col. Andrew Erwin, had built a large, successful mercantile business in Asheville, North Carolina, in partnership with his brother-in-law, James Patton.[4] When Colonel Erwin retired from the business, the Erwin family moved to rural Tennessee, where they operated a dairy business.

On October 10, 1823, Henry Clay received a letter from Tennessee Governor William Carroll saying that he had consulted a number of gentlemen who had known James Erwin from his childhood. He reported that Erwin had "acquired great credit . . . for extricating himself from the pecuniary embarrassments of a large mercantile business in which he was engaged in some years ago. His connections in this state, in Georgia, and the Carolinas are as extensive and respectable as that of any family of which I have knowledge in the United States."[5] Although Clay's reservations continued, he gave his approval for James Erwin and Anne Brown Clay to be married on October 21, 1823.

Clay wanted his children to have their own homes in Lexington and encouraged James Erwin

Figure 4.1 The Woodlands, the Erwin Home in Lexington. *J. Winston Coleman Kentuckiana Collection, Transylvania University*

to purchase the "Woodlands" on 108 acres of land (now Woodland Park in Lexington). A sizable farm house had been built on the property, located on the south side of the main street of Lexington, closer to town than Ashland but within easy walking distance of Henry Clay's home. Clay advanced the funds to pay for the property and took the precaution of placing the property in a trust that benefited his daughter during her lifetime and, in the event of her death, specified that the title would revert to her children.[6]

After the property was purchased, the Erwin family added several distinctive features to the house that made it unusual for the area. They built octagonal flankers at the four corners of the house with the front flankers linked to a rounded entrance hall similar to the front hall at Ashland. A balustrade encircling the flat roof recalled the architecture in New Orleans, where the couple spent their winters.[7]

James Erwin did not practice law, but instead focused on land trading and commodities speculation, spending most of his time in New Orleans. To finance property investments in Louisiana, Texas, and Mississippi, he used money borrowed from his family, his wife, and the Clay family.[8] Anne reported to her father that her husband's speculations were doing well.

The Woodlands April 11

My dear Father

. . .Mr. Erwin having made some pretty little speculations this winter I feel more disposed to indulge in a little extravagance. Mama need feel no uneasiness on my account as I have never been in better health in my life than I have enjoyed for the last six months. The boys come out generally to dine with me every day; they complain a little of eating at Mr Pince's but from their appearances they have not been starved; I never saw John [fifth and youngest son] look as fat as he does and James [Henry Clay's fourth son] is constantly laughing at him for eating so much. John comes out every Saturday and stays until Sunday morning with us. I was at Ashland on Sunday, M. Hall [Miss Sarah Hall, the long-time Yorkshire housekeeper for the Clay family] has already had the house cleaned & put in order, and everything is going on as well as usual on the whole farm. The children join me in love to Mama and yourself.[9]

While James Erwin stayed in New Orleans, Anne spent most of her time raising a growing family at the Woodlands. A child was born each year beginning in 1825. Andrew Eugene Erwin was the fifth child, born in October 1830, at the Woodlands. At the time of Eugene's birth, his mother's health had become a problem, she seemed to be suffering from tuberculosis. When Eugene was five, his mother died suddenly at her home on December 10, 1835, as a result of what was described as the rupture of a blood vessel following childbirth. Shortly thereafter, James Erwin wrote to Henry Clay in Washington:

I feel myself scarcely equal to the task which my duty imposes, that of writing you at this time, and speaking of the late dreadful calamity with which it has pleased God to afflict us—by which, at the same fatal blow, has been taken from you a daughter, unequaled in filial devotion and love, and from me a wife, the most devoted, kind and virtuous, with which man was ever blessed. . . . Mrs. Clay at once kindly proposed taking charge of all [of the children] . . .and the plan is now to leave the three youngest at Ashland. . . . I hope I will hear from you very soon after I reach New Orleans.[10]

Clay was devastated by the loss of his daughter and hardly functioned for weeks following the news of her death.[11] James Erwin cared for his two oldest boys in New Orleans, while Eugene and his brother and sister moved to Ashland to be reared by the grandparents. The two families worked closely to manage the upbringing of the Erwin children, with James visiting Lexington each summer and Henry Clay traveling to New Orleans on several occasions.

For a period of time, James Erwin retired from his business. He wrote the following in response to a request by Col. William H. Russell to invest in land in Missouri.

New Orleans, January 12th 1836

Dear Sir

I reached this city yesterday and found your letter of the 24th Nov which will account to you for the delay in receiving an answer. I was detained in Kentucky much later than usual by the severest of all afflictions. The illness and death of my wife more dear to me than life itself. This unexpected & melancholy event has rendered me unfit for any kind of business. My hopes are all destroyed. My present plan is to withdraw from all kind of business and to devote myself to my children. I may not be able to do so, it may be necessary for me in order to escape my own reflections if left alone to engage actively in business—but I will try the first.

I am fully aware of the immense prospects that can be derived from such investments and I assure you there is no man with whom I would sooner engage than yourself—I have

> been operating largely and profitably in Arkansas in the manner proposed by you. I shall now wind up my speculations there and elsewhere. . . .[12]

Erwin's retirement was short lived. After he formed an investment company for the purpose of commodity and land speculation, Henry Clay invested with him in a number of land speculations in Louisiana and cosigned large loans to finance the transactions. In 1840, there was a decline in the New Orleans economy and several banking companies failed. Clay was concerned because he had borrowed $40,000 jointly with James Erwin from John Jacob Astor in New York requiring annual payments of principal and interest, with the loan due in 1847.[13] Payments were not made on schedule by Erwin so Clay had to arrange for a separate note with extended terms. Clay also learned that Erwin had borrowed $52,000 from his children by mortgaging the Woodlands, which Clay had placed in trust for their future benefit.[14]

Erwin's reputation in Lexington suffered from rumors about a relationship with a dance hall singer in New Orleans and the nonpayment of trade obligations. A dispute developed over the ownership of the Woodlands.[15] Laws governing property rights favored the husband's position after a woman married—indeed, property held by a woman was transferred to her husband's name at the time of marriage. James Erwin's creditors took the position that Anne Clay's marriage superseded Henry Clay's trust agreement covering the Woodlands, and they had a right to sell the property to cover James Erwin's debts. Clay represented Eugene Erwin and his brothers and sister in the court battle.

Erwin's immediate financial difficulties were resolved in 1843, when he married a twenty-one-year-old local woman from a prominent Lexington family, Margaret Julia Johnson.[16] Eugene Erwin maintained a lively correspondence with his stepmother, Margaret. She called Eugene "her loving son in spirit if not in flesh and blood" and urged him not to overindulge in alcohol and gambling like his brothers. Her entertaining letters were filled with gossip about the Clay and Erwin families, though her letter dated August 8, 1851, must have upset him.

> Your grandfather [Henry Clay] has proven my greatest enemy under the guise of love for you all, which he had never shown, and I do not believe he feels, he is trying to deprive me of every dollar left me. You remember the judgment which Pa [James Erwin] holds on the Woodlands of $6,000 which is just. Pa assumed the debt years ago to prevent the place being sold [which] I acquired. Your Grandfather pretends to think it a fraudulent transaction and is trying to deprive me of it. . . . He has in the last two days filed a Bill to rent the place this August. . . . . Lucretia [Eugene's sister] has told lies all over town about me.[17]

When James Erwin died in 1851 and left a bankrupt estate, the Woodlands was sold the following year. Despite being in ill health, Henry Clay was able to obtain court approval to have the proceeds of approximately $40,000, distributed to his daughter Anne's children. Eugene Erwin received a sum of about $10,000, enough to marry and support a new career.

After their visit to Lexington, the Russell-Erwin party traveled to the Russell home near Fulton, Missouri, where Eugene and Josephine were married in the Catholic Church on July 10, 1853.[18] Eugene Erwin was determined to overcome his father's reputation by recovering the land his estate claimed while building a new life and career on the frontier in Missouri.

Eugene and Josephine Erwin moved to Independence, Missouri, where Eugene planned to work in a mercantile business supporting the western emigration. This town, located on the Missouri River on the western border of Missouri, was called the "Queen City of the Trails." On the edge of America's frontier in the 1850s, it was the staging area for thousands of gold rush travelers. Travelers on three trails west; the Santa Fe, California, and Oregon were outfitted in Independence. Mercantilists, blacksmiths, wagon makers, and freighters formed a hub of trading activity that brought wealth to the community. The first railroad west of the Mississippi linked the center of town, Independence Square, to a landing on the river where steamboats and barges delivered goods from the east. Located on this square was the finest hotel west of St. Louis, the Jones Hotel.

Colonel and Mrs. Russell also moved to Independence in the fall 1853, and the Russell and Erwin families resided at the Jones Hotel. It was owned by Lewis Jones, a Santa Fe freighter originally from Culpeper County, Virginia. Jones most likely was an old friend of Colonel Russell, whose family had also lived in Culpeper County. The hotel was well known because Kit Carson and his trail finders stayed there, and it became a favorite of many travelers. An early newspaper reported "the Jones Hotel is quite a favorite resort of youth and beauty of both Independence and Kansas City," but it was also reported that some of the customers traveling west were fairly rough. To protect against fire and to provide privacy, the two principal floors contained rooms divided by walls two feet thick supported by a heavy stone foundation.[19]

The Erwin family was expanding. In 1854 Josephine gave birth to their first child, Lucretia (Lula) Clay Erwin, and they moved to their own home in the small village of Harrisonville, Missouri, twenty miles south of Independence.[20] Colonel Russell and Zaenett had also moved to a farm south of Independence in Cass County, and Russell continued to spend much of his time traveling in Missouri and to Washington, D. C., to promote the Whig cause while seeking a government appointment. On March 4, 1855, Zaenett wrote to her sister-in-law Sarah Russell in Lexington:

> Mr. Erwin has also purchased in Cass County about eight miles from our farm; Jo and sweet Lula have been with me all winter, while her husband was attending to making improvements necessary to enable him to take his family. Jo left me about two weeks since for her new home; she did not expect to be pleased. In a few days she wrote to me that although not quite so enthusiastic an admirer of Cass as Mr. E., she was delighted to feel busy at her own home and was very contented. Lula has improved very much since you saw her. I never saw a brighter face than she has, and everyone that sees her thinks her very pretty. I feel her parents are too fond of her; were they to lose Lula, it would be a severe trial to both, particularly her Mother.[21]

Two other daughters were born in Missouri—Zaenett (Nettie) Erwin in 1857 and Mary (Mamie) Webster Erwin in 1861. Because of the high rate of infant and childhood mortality, new parents were urged not to become too attached to their children or to "spoil" them. Josephine's only correspondence during this period in her scrapbook was some friendly advice on child rearing from a friend in San Francisco:

> February 8th (ca. 1857)
>
> Dear Mrs. Erwin,
>
> I hardly remember who were your friends in California—and it has all changed so much that you would hardly recognize any locality—San Francisco grows so rapidly—Sacramento more slowly but still greatly altered.

> I would like to speak to you seriously about your children—I have three and so think myself competent to give advice—and what can I say that you and your husband do not already know. It seems to me that you are "making to yourself idols" and laying up—oh it may be such a fearful disappointment to yourself. I do not speak merely from a religious point of view though that is sufficiently serious, but for the children's own sake—for their future I would ask you seriously as a friend do you sufficiently guard them against the effects of your own fondship (sic). Do you yield to their present demands too implicitly—pardon me for seeming to intrude my opinions—I mean nothing but what friendship might permit. The subject is one of such vast importance—nothing less than forming a character which nothing can ever change or annihilate that it well deserves our most constant endeavors to mould it aright.
>
> I have two little girls and one boy and the difficulty I find in guiding them always wisely must be my apology for pressing the subject on you.
>
> Very truly yours
>
> Georgie Cornwall[22]

Eugene Erwin became actively involved in land trading. He purchased a 1,286-acre farm near Clinton, Missouri, fifty miles to the southwest of Independence. He also made land purchases in Alabama, Tennessee, and Mississippi with his brother, Henry Clay Erwin, and uncle, Andrew Erwin. To pursue the land claims of his father's estate in Louisiana and Texas, Eugene filed lawsuits on behalf of the family against the current residents of the land.[23]

Colonel Russell began to spend more time in Kansas to investigate new opportunities to practice law and support the Whig Party on this new frontier. Zaenett Russell stayed at their home in Missouri. The Erwin family and Zaenett Russell returned to the Jones Hotel in Independence when Cass County became a center for conflict between pro-and-antislavery groups and the base for a violent rebel group called Quantrill's raiders. The 1860 Census in Jackson County, Missouri, listed the Eugene Erwin family living in the Jones Hotel in Independence with Zaenett Russell who had separated from her husband.

Eugene Erwin augmented the capital he received in the sale of the Woodlands property in Lexington; he was listed with real estate valued at $6,500 and personal property worth $15,000, a substantial sum of money at that time. Zaenett owned real estate worth $2,000 and personal property worth $5,000.[24]

On December 20, 1860, South Carolina seceded from the Union and other southern states followed. In February 1861, a state convention was held in St. Louis to decide Missouri's position in the conflict. The results found "no adequate cause to impel Missouri to dissolve her connection with the Federal Union," but a majority also opposed joining the Union effort to go to war with the seceding states.

John C. Frémont, one of four major generals appointed by President Abraham Lincoln at the onset of the Civil War, was assigned command of the Western Department headquartered in St. Louis in July 1861. Frémont focused Union forces at Cairo, Illinois, to control steamship traffic traveling down the Ohio River destined for Missouri, and as a result shipments to Independence were disrupted. Attacks by bands of men called Jayhawkers, who favored the Confederate cause, shifted trade from Independence and Kansas City to the safety of Fort Leavenworth.

Without consulting President Lincoln, General Frémont declared martial law in Missouri and issued an emancipation proclamation freeing all slaves in the state. Lincoln was furious, because this order offended border states whose support he needed. He relieved Frémont of all duties. Frémont's actions created ill-will among the young men in Independence, many of whom volunteered for the local militia organized to defend the state against Union aggression.[25]

Josephine was strongly opposed to her husband taking sides in the conflict. On May 14, 1861, Eugene was in Denver selling corn from his farm when he wrote to his wife:

> You may set your mind at rest about my engaging in the present political difficulties. Although my feeling would prompt me to rally to the standard of the Confederate States, my duty to my family restrains me. I am not willing to risk my life in the present unsettled condition of my business. My family and their happiness is all that I have to live for and so long as my wife continues to be what she is, I shall esteem it my first duty to consult her wishes and happiness.[26]

Not long after he wrote this letter, Eugene Erwin began to feel, as did many Missourians, that he must defend the state from intervention, and in early August 1861, he entered the Missouri militia. Eugene's training at the Kentucky Military Institute had provided him with a good knowledge of military strategy and leadership. After he led a local skirmish with forces at Wilson's Creek on August 10, Erwin was promoted from private to first lieutenant. Believing he could contribute more in the regular Confederate army, he resigned from the militia and joined Col. Thomas H. Rosser, who was organizing men from Missouri for a Confederate force that came to be known as Rosser's Battalion. Erwin was commissioned a first lieutenant in the Confederate Missouri Infantry just before the Battle of Elkhorn Tavern.[27]

It must have troubled Josephine that her husband decided to fight for a Confederate cause that she opposed. Later in her life Josephine wrote:

> Rabid politicians—not statesmen—on both sides, now stand responsible before the world for the woes . . . the South was far from being unanimous for secession and with few exceptions, incompetence was characteristic of the leaders, notably the West Point rubbish, whose loss to the Union was a gain, and infection for military glory, to "win big battles," to inscribe the commander's name on the "imperishable roll of honor," caused a waste of life unparalleled—if this was glory, it was glory of the kind the South had not the means to maintain.
>
> But if one man was ever more conspicuously distinguished above all men who have ever lived for bigotry, obstinacy and mistakes, that man was Jefferson Davis. (Extract from a Southern newspaper: "Shall the cause fail because Mr. Davis is incompetent?" The people of the Confederacy must answer this plain question at once, or they are lost).[28]

After the battle of Elkhorn Tavern, Eugene's battalion was sent south to Arkansas and Mississippi to reinforce Gen. Albert Sidney Johnston after the fall of Forts Henry and Donelson. Union forces under the command of Gen. Ulysses S. Grant were attempting to take control of the Mississippi River to split the Confederacy and cut off the supply of Confederate troops. There were skirmishes between Union and Confederate forces in the towns surrounding the key river port and defensive position of the Confederate army at Vicksburg, Mississippi.[29]

Before her husband left for Mississippi, Josephine inquired if she could volunteer for nursing duties as had many other wives of Federal and Confederate soldiers. Eugene was strongly opposed, and Josephine, who had a newborn daughter to care for, decided against volunteering. To provide what help she could, she knitted seventy-five pairs of wool socks that were sent to soldiers fighting in Mississippi.[30]

Eugene continued to work on the lawsuit to recover properties claimed by his father's estate. The suit to remove "squatters" on what he believed was his father's land had progressed to the highest court in Louisiana. His attorney in New Orleans, Gustavus Schmidt, wrote to Eugene on December 5, 1861, that "I expect a final decision of the Supreme Court on the 14th inst. & I presume that in 8 or 10 days afterwards I shall be able to effect a settlement with the Curator of your father's estate."[31] Disappointment followed when his lawsuit and other pending civil actions were suspended due to the more urgent business of the war of succession, and the case was never resolved.

On May 15, 1862, Erwin was promoted to lieutenant colonel in charge of a battalion, the Sixth Missouri Infantry.[32] On July 4, he issued the following Circular to his men.

> July 4th 1862 "Circular" To The Officers and Soldiers of Erwin's Batt.
>
> It has been customary upon this the anniversary of our first Independence to meet together with our wives, mothers and sisters and commemorate the day with feasting and social enjoyments. That blessed privilege is on this day denied us, but let us unite in doing that which will call forth thanks and prayers and alleviate the sufferings of those brave soldiers who are now bleeding and suffering from wounds in the late battle near Richmond and the remembrance of this day will be as sweet in after years as any that has passed.
>
> I desire that the Capt. of the different Companies composing my Batt. will prepare Subscription Lists and give each individual member of their respective commands an opportunity to contribute their mite for this object.
>
> The Several Lists and sums of money will be returned to my Head Quar. to be forwarded to the Medical Director of the Army at Richmond, Va.
>
> Eugene Erwin, Lt. Col. Comm., Erwin's Batt.[33]

The result of this July 4 project was a $2,350 gift from Erwin's men to the medical service of the Confederate army in Richmond. This project was widely covered in the southern press and came to the attention of the Confederate government. A few weeks later, three more companies were added to form a regiment, and Erwin was promoted to colonel in charge, Sixth Missouri Infantry CSA.[34] Confederate President Jefferson Davis, who had written a letter of introduction for Eugene Erwin when he traveled to California, may have endorsed his rapid promotion.[35]

During the summer of 1862 Union Gen. John M. Schofield outlined a new program to strike against local rebels in Missouri by occupying one town in each county of the state. Civilians including women in each town were interviewed about their loyalties, and if they could not prove their allegiance to the United States, they were fined and banished from the state in order to "make an example." The fines were levied to support the widows of Federal soldiers. Hundreds of women in Missouri were officially fined and banished; thousands more left Missouri when their homes were burned and they were threatened with banishment.[36]

The fact that Josephine opposed the fighting did not matter to Federal officers in Jackson County, who assumed that all the wives of Confederate officers were traitors. Erwin's fellow officer Capt. James E. Payne reported in a newspaper article that Josephine was "banished" from Independence in the spring of 1863 and given a period of time to settle her affairs and leave the state.[37]

Josephine wanted to rejoin her husband, but it had been over a year since she had received any communication from him. There was no mail service from the Vicksburg area, and she feared that he was in a hospital or had been killed or captured.

She may have considered an offer to move her family to Lexington. Mrs. Lucretia Clay, had moved to a large new home with her son, John M. Clay, and invited Josephine and her family to live with them in their new home until the war was over.[38]

Josephine was with her mother and three young daughters at the Jones Hotel in Independence when a man introduced himself to the hotel manager and asked to deliver a letter to Mrs. Erwin. She met him in the lobby, and he handed her a letter. She immediately recognized that it was from her husband and asked where he was located. She learned that her husband had been in a hospital in Holly Springs, Mississippi, with a serious foot injury but had now resumed his command in the area of Grand Gulf, Mississippi.[39] Josephine opened the letter.

> My dear Wife
>
> There are many things that I would like to write to you, but the uncertainty of this letter reaching its destination prevents me. I hope that you have not suffered for the necessaries of life although you have undoubtedly had a great many hardships to endure. I have been very prudent and economical with my pay in order that I might have something at the termination of the War.
>
> You will be pleased to learn that my conduct has been such as an Officer & Soldier as to elicit the highest encomiums from my Commanding Generals. I have endeavored to build up a reputation of which my Angel Wife and darling Children would be proud and I believe I have succeeded. God grant that I may live to enjoy it with them. We have had many trials to undergo and many hardships to endure but none half so great as the separation from you but through them all I have felt the proud consciousness that my wife although subjected to trials that would try the spirit of an angel would pass through them all with spirits unbroken and honor untarnished and this knowledge was sweeter and more consoling to me than the applause of friends, or increase of honors. I resigned a Lieut. Col's. Commission in the State Service to enter the Confederate Service as a Private. I was soon elected 1st Lieut. then Lieut. Col. in command of a Battalion and afterwards Col. in Command of one of the best Regiments in the Service, and after the Battle of Corinth I was strongly urged by Genl. Price and other officers for the appointment of Brig. Genl. Truly this career is brilliant enough to satisfy the most grasping ambition but what does it amount to when I cannot have you with me to enjoy with me the pleasure it would otherwise afford me.
>
> When shall we meet again, that is the important question now. From every indication I am firmly persuaded that the War will close by the 1st of June. The dissensions in the north, the demoralization of the Federal Army, the state of their finances, all indicate it. Deserters are coming in every day by the hundreds and all agree as to the utter demoralization of

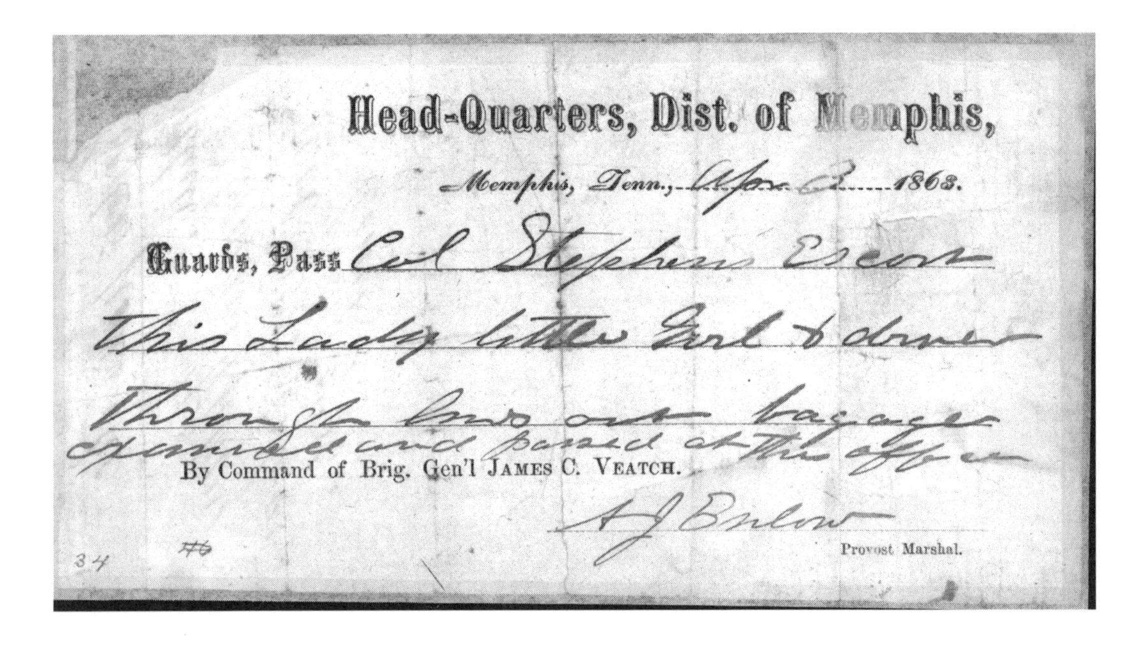

Head-Quarters, Dist. of Memphis,

Memphis, Tenn., Apr 2 1863.

Guards, Pass Col Stephens Escort
This Lady little Girl & driver
Through the lines our baggage
examined and passed at this office

By Command of Brig. Gen'l JAMES C. VEATCH.

Provost Marshal.

Fig. 4.2 Guards Pass from the Command of Brig. Gen. James C. Veatch, April 3, 1863. *UK*

the Federal Army. It will be impossible for them to take Vicksburg and without it their army cannot penetrate the state of Mississippi. Our army is in excellent condition. My Regiment is here at the present time as a reserve to thrust to Vicksburg which is only 40 miles or Port Hudson as the emergencies may require.

I wish you to answer this letter immediately and address the letter to me under cover to the gentleman who takes it and who will send you directions where to direct it to him. If you will address letters to me under cover to W. C. Potter, Memphis Tennessee they will be forwarded to me. If you are at all comfortably situated you had better not attempt to come to me now as it is so late in the winter and there is a probability that we will be kept constantly on the move in the spring.

Your Brother George was wounded also at Corinth but has entirely recovered. He behaved very gallantly. Ten thousand kisses to the Children and my kind love to your Mother.

Col. Eugene Erwin
6th Mo Infy, 1st Brigade Price's Divn
Army of the Mississippi[40]

Despite the risk of traveling during wartime, Josephine wanted to join her husband in Grand Gulf, Mississippi, as soon as possible. She arranged for a wagon and drivers and headed east to St. Louis. Josephine took her nine-year-old daughter, Lula, with her leaving the two younger children with their grandmother. In St. Louis, she booked passage on a steamship to Memphis and arranged for a "Guards Pass" to be issued to permit her to pass through the Union lines. This pass was signed by Brig. Gen. James C. Veatch in Memphis on April 3, 1863.

Josephine and Lula rode in an open wagon to Grand Gulf, Mississippi, camping where she could with Confederate soldiers. Josephine later wrote:

> The sight was indeed one to occasion surprise, and stands alone in the history of warfare. A woman in a pony phaeton was driving between the hostile lines. . . . She did not seem alarmed and driving slowly, was looking curiously around. Intently watching her were thousands of eyes from which all the fierceness of battle had died away, leaving only anxious apprehensions. "What if some stray bullet fired accidentally, or at random, should find its way to the occupant of that little carriage?" Breathing almost ceased until she had passed from sight.[41]

Colonel Erwin received a note from fellow officer, J. Murdock:

> Mrs. Erwin & Lula were seen by a friend of mine last night at ten o'clock, encamped with the army at Grindstone Ford. Mr. Ratterson brought word of their safety after the battle, and they seemed cheerful and hopeful when they left us at 6 o'clock.
>
> Respectfully yr friend, J Murdock
>
> 11 ½ o'clock Saturday. We will be glad to share our home with your family; as long as we have one.[42]

In Grand Gulf, Mississippi, Josephine was reunited with her husband, and she stayed with him throughout the Vicksburg Campaign.

Chapter 5

Tragedy at Vicksburg

And legends of glory will never depart
From the valiant soldier with a tender heart.[1]

The Confederate fortress at Vicksburg with a commanding defensive position on the Mississippi River had become the focus of Federal army plans. President Lincoln told General Grant that "Vicksburg is the key . . . the war can never be brought to a close until the key is in our pocket." Numerous attempts to attack Vicksburg had failed, but Grant was being reinforced with additional troops which would eventually grow to seventy thousand men, and he had developed a new plan to approach the city from the South. In the spring 1863, Grant's army crossed the Mississippi River south of Vicksburg at Bruinsburg, Mississippi and began offensive operations against the Confederate army at Port Gibson.[2]

On May 1, 1863, Colonel Erwin's regiment was ordered to leave the trenches at Grand Gulf and join the fighting in Port Gibson. He led 520 men to a position holding the left wing of the Confederate force within twenty yards of the enemy. For one and a half hours, they stopped the Union advance, but when reinforcements failed to arrive and ammunition was exhausted, Erwin withdrew his troops. In the course of the fighting, he suffered another severe foot injury.[3]

After the defeat at Port Gibson, Gen. John C. Pemberton, commander of the Confederate army in Mississippi, moved his forces to the area of Jackson, Mississippi, but after defeats in skirmishes at Raymond, Champion's Hill, and Big Black River, he ordered a withdrawal into the fortress at Vicksburg. Injuries forced Eugene to give up his command, and he made the retreat to Vicksburg in a horse-drawn ambulance, accompanied by Josephine and Lula.[4] Josephine described what happened next through the character Geraldine Southampton in *Uncle Phil.*

> About sundown an ambulance was sent . . .for their removal. At the suspension bridge spanning the Bayou Pierre their progress was almost barred by the crowd of non-combatants hurrying across, volubly announcing their patriotism and their intention to stay in the Confederacy so long as there was an inch of it left.
>
> The officer, whose duty it was to burn the bridge to retard the enemy, was loudly berating them, accusing the men of cowardice for not being in arms. "And so long as you don't fight," he cried hotly, "it makes no difference where you are, whether in the Confederacy or in hell!" Seeing Miss Southampton, whom he knew by sight, his angry manner changed

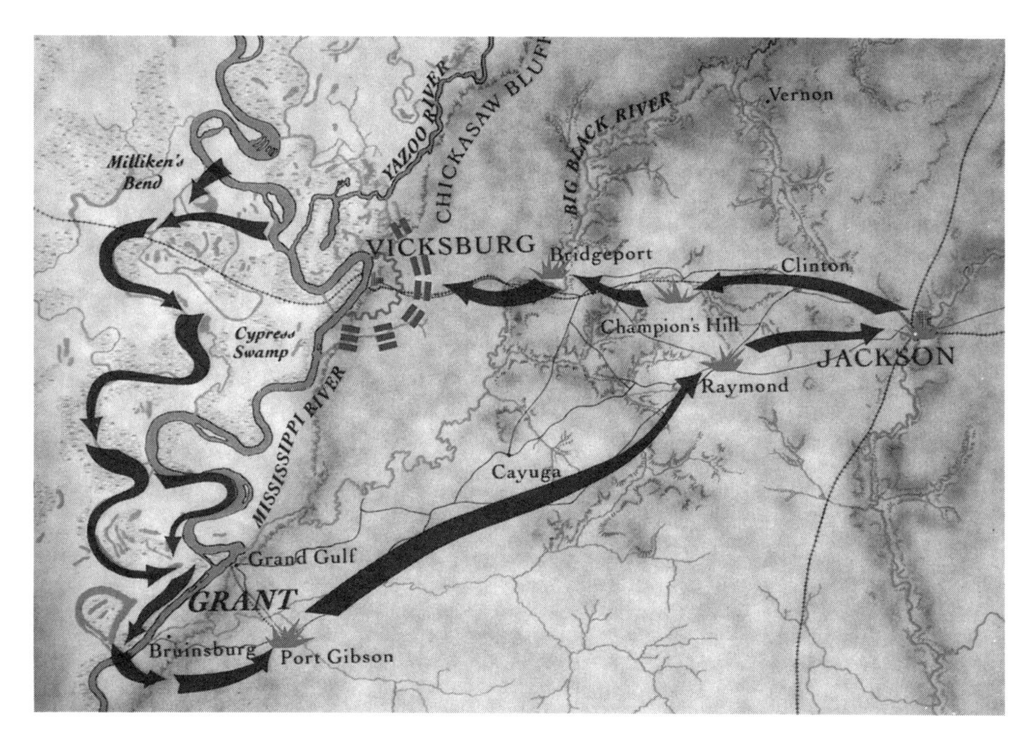

Fig.5.1 Map of the Civil War Fighting Near Vicksburg. *U. S. Army Historical Institute*

to polite consideration. "Here, madam, this way, pass right over." Then he ordered a squad of soldiers he had with him to form into line and "Keep these people back with your bayonets." A barrel of turpentine had been placed on the bridge and, dipping into it with a pitcher, the woodwork was soon drenched with the flammable fluid, and Geraldine Southampton was scarcely over when a match was applied and a bright light briefly illuminated the gathering twilight.

On the third day afterward, Miss Southampton in her somewhat roundabout journey came across the Sixth Regiment of Missouri Infantry when they were taking their ten minutes' halt. This regiment had been taken out of the trenches at Grand Gulf, double-quick marched eight miles and precipitated into the battle before Port Gibson, and were the rear-guard of the Confederate army in full retreat. With little rest and food this fatiguing duty taxed to the utmost their courage and physical endurance. At the welcome halt of ten minutes every two hours, down they would drop, right where they stood, not to lose an instant of the much needed rest. A mounted courier had just come up and was reading aloud an army dispatch which claimed a brilliant victory for the Southern forces in Virginia. The reading was listened to in silence—these soldiers had grown distrustful of the brilliant victories claimed at opportune times—until the mention was made that Stonewall Jackson had lost an arm. "I wish to heaven," said one of the weary soldiers, slowly raising his head, "that they would send that arm here to take command of us." It seldom falls to the lot of an officer to be as universally disbelieved in as was Pemberton . . . .[5]

5.2 Underground Houses in Vicksburg, June 1863. *Vicksburg National Military Park*

Despite the use of overwhelming force, the Federal assaults failed to penetrate well fortified Confederate positions surrounding Vicksburg. General Grant decided to lay siege to Vicksburg on May 26 and ordered his army to surround the town with troops and blockade the Mississippi River with Federal gunboats and iron-clads. The white tents of Grant's army were seen in all directions around Vicksburg.

Weeks went by and the Confederate defenders and town civilians were subjected to continuous probing attacks and bombardment. The noise was intense as shells, finishing the seven-mile trip from Federal positions, burst continuously on Vicksburg. "There goes a whistling dick" was the cry as the shells passed. To avoid the shells, many people lived underground. Deep cuts through the yellow clay were used to carve out rooms, and some were even decorated with carpets and furnished.[6] Josephine and her daughter lived above ground in a tented area near the temporary hospital where her husband recovered from his wounds.[7] Josephine worked as a nurse to the injured.

Josephine wrote:

> The land fighting began for the possession of Vicksburg ("We have come to knock at the back door," facetiously remarked Colonel Johnston, of Grant's staff); and all that long May day was passed in the hospital where the wounded men were brought from the field of battle, wounded in every imaginable fashion, from the little round hole—not so bad to look at—which soldiers know so well. No surgeon's sentence is needed to tell them that the man will never march again in this world. And how sickening are those ugly hurts, rent and jagged by the canister.[8]

Just across the entrance to Fort Hill, an additional defensive work had been constructed. Behind the fortification, Colonel Erwin's Sixth Missouri Regiment waited in reserve.[9]

Erwin was in a temporary hospital when one of the officers in his regiment approached and told him that they would soon be engaging Federal troops. He immediately left his sickbed, and with Josephine's assistance, dressed in his uniform and sword. Josephine described the scene in *Uncle Phil.*

> He was a self-contained man, rarely showing outward sign of his emotions, yet his face was white with pain when he faced her to speak farewell. He clasped her hand, his words coming slowly—perhaps I may never look on your sweet face again—but God bless you forever and forever."
>
> "Good-bye, darling. . . ."[10]

Fig. 5.3 Col. Eugene Erwin

He left the hospital and rode his horse toward Fort Hill. Suddenly, at 4:30 p.m. the entire hill exploded and a great cloud of dust flew skyward. The sound broke window panes in the city of Vicksburg. Federal troops had dug under the fortification and set off explosives. The main tunnel was forty-five feet in length and two branches were run out on each side for fifteen feet. Gen. Louis Hebert, in charge of Confederate troops in the area, sensing that mining was in progress, had taken the precaution of withdrawing his forces behind a defensive position nearby, while six Mississippians were working on a counter mining effort. They were buried alive in the earthworks.[11]

The explosion created a crater, but did not completely destroy the parapet protecting the Confederate position. Federal troops from the Forty-fifth Illinois Infantry rushed into the crater and attempted to cross the parapet. Fierce hand-to-hand combat ensued with the Third Louisiana Regiment, which began to fall back.

General Hebert's battle notes explain what happened when Colonel Erwin reached the Third Louisiana position: "he dismounted, drew a sword, and yelled 'come on boys, don't let the third get ahead of you!' He led a charge that repulsed the Federal assault."

At 6 p.m., Erwin, believing that the Federal forces were falling back, again led a charge over the parapet to drive the Union men from the crater. He immediately became the target of sharp-shooters. A minié ball struck him in the chest on the left side in the area of the heart, killing him instantly. The counterattack was ended and there followed charge after charge by Erwin's men to the top of the parapet heaving hand grenades and shells with lighted fuses into the crater. General Grant, realizing that the assault had failed, called for a retreat. During the battle, 34 Federal soldiers were killed and 209 injured, while Confederate losses totaled 21 killed and 73 wounded.[12]

At midnight, a squad of Missourians took the body of Colonel Erwin to the site of the regiment's camp in Stouts Bayou. With Josephine and Lula in attendance, he was buried in the soft earth in a wooden coffin with a plain board, roughly lettered to mark the spot. W. M. Patterson, the Chaplain of the Sixth Missouri Infantry wrote Eugene Erwin's obituary, and it was printed on a yellow ribbon given to the Confederate troops:

> Another brave and noble spirit has fallen. On Thursday evening, June 25th, Col. Eugene Erwin, of the 6th Regiment Missouri Vols., was killed while mounted upon the works, with a view to leading a charge against the enemy. He was struck with a minié ball which passed through his body, killing him instantly.
>
> For several weeks previous to his death, his health had been delicate, and at times compelled his absence from the field. During the siege of this place, he had more than once been driven to his bed; and on the day of his death, he was out contrary to the advice and urging of his friends, feeling, as he said, that it was his duty, so long as he could stand, to stand at this post. No one felt more than he did the importance of every man's discharging his duty—no one did more to discharge it. . . .
>
> But he has fallen—fallen at his post, defending the cause of justice and truth. At midnight's hour, amid the roar of cannon and whistling of the enemy's balls, we bore him gently and laid him in the soldier's humble grave, where he shall rest in peace till he is called forth to his reward in the resurrection morn. . . .
>
> He leaves a wife and three sweet little girls to mourn his loss. May our Heavenly Father sustain and comfort them in their sad bereavement, and grant them all a happy reunion in the Heavenly world, where sorrows and separations, wars and death are known no more.[13]

Erwin was thirty-two years old when he died at the siege of Vicksburg.

One account of the battle claimed that Colonel Erwin acted in an irresponsible manner by leading his men in a charge that had little chance for success. This was refuted by Capt. John Payne, Sixth Missouri Infantry CSA, who reported that Erwin was an inspirational hero. The story of Erwin's charge in defense of Vicksburg was taught in Vicksburg schools and is featured as one of the first sto-

Fig. 5.5 Monument to Col. Eugene Erwin. *Vicksburg National Military Park.*

ries presented in the current tour of the Vicksburg National Military Park. He was honored, as were other senior officers on both sides of the conflict, with a monument located near the scene of his final battle, the Third Louisiana Redan.[14]

Josephine and Lula were provided with a special guard for protection. The daily ration had been cut to one biscuit and a bit of ham, and they suffered from lack of sleep and hunger. Civilians had resorted to eating birds and rats to sustain life. A week after Erwin's death, General Pemberton met with General Grant and asked for the terms of surrender. The Vicksburg campaign had ended. The surrender of 30,000 Confederate troops was the largest Union victory up to that time, and the fall of Vicksburg cut off the Confederacy from vital sources of food, men, and transport on the Mississippi River. President Lincoln commented that the Mississippi again flowed "unvexed to the sea."

The formal surrender took place on July 4, 1863, and it would require a national crisis during the Second World War before the Fourth of July would be celebrated again in Vicksburg. The terms called for a single Federal division to take possession of the city: "As soon as paroles can be signed by the officers and men, [Confederate soldiers] will be allowed to march out with officers taking side-arms and clothing and cavalry officers one horse each. The rank and file will be allowed all their clothing, but no other property." According to Grant's memoir of the siege, the two armies fraternized as if they had been fighting for the same cause.[15]

Josephine met with the officers and troops of Erwin's regiment. To help the wounded, she desperately searched for medicine to treat injuries. Sgt. Lucien McDowell wrote to her that: "We have no Spits-Camphor as the Yankees have entirely failed to supply us with Spits of any kind since we have been in Vicksburg. I send some Gum hoping it may answer the purpose."[16]

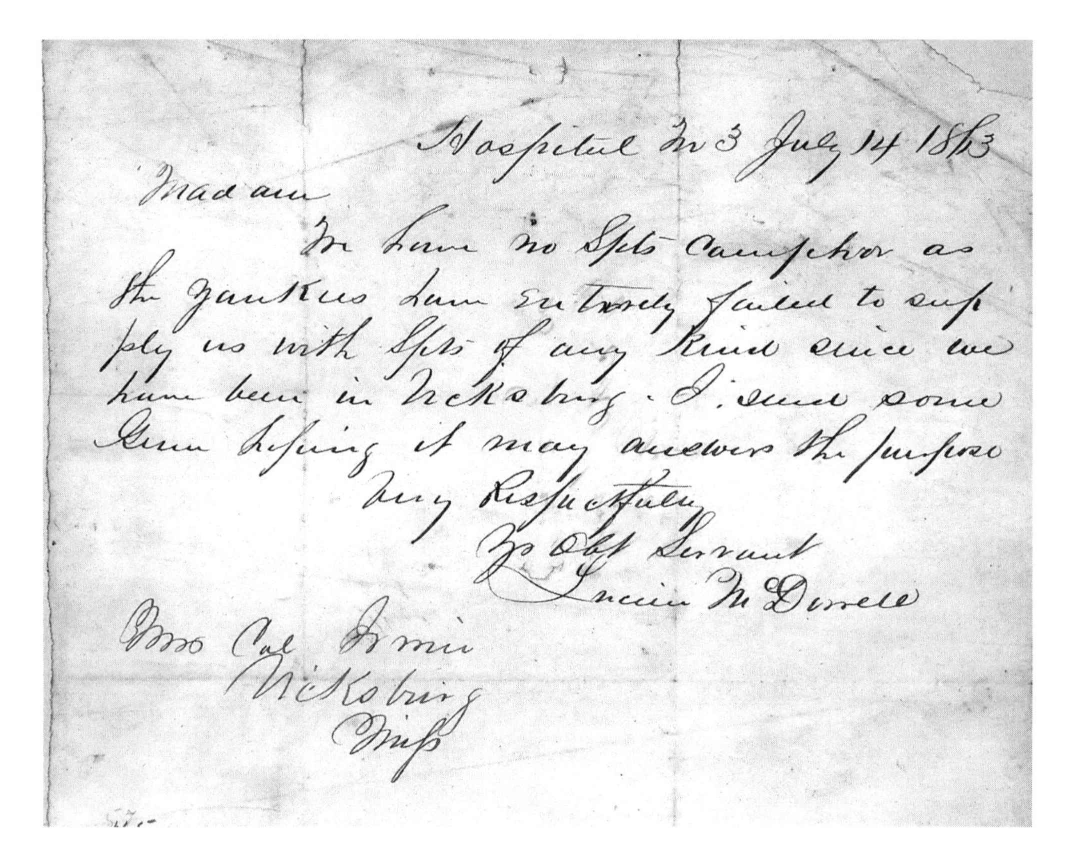

Hospital No 3 July 14 1863

Madam

We have no Spts Camphor as the Yankees have entirely failed to supply us with Spts of any kind since we have been in Vicksburg. I send some Gum hoping it may answers the purpose

Very Respectfully
Yr Obt Servant
Lucien McDowell

Mrs Col Erwin
Vicksburg
Miss

Fig. 5.6 Josephine Erwin's Request for Spits Camphor. *UK*

Lt. Edwin H. Hickman, a company commander of the Sixth Missouri who had lost an arm, asked Josephine about her plans for returning to Missouri. She revealed to him that she was pregnant and needed help. A few days later, Hickman saw Col. Thomas L. Fletcher, a Union Missouri infantry officer and former prisoner of war whom Hickman had guarded. Hickman told Fletcher that Mrs. Erwin was pregnant with the great-grandchild of Henry Clay. At 10 a.m. on July 18, Fletcher, who would later become governor of Missouri, led Josephine and Hickman to Lum House, a twenty-six room mansion on Main Street in Vicksburg, where General Grant made his headquarters.[17]

Grant was with his adjutant and a major general, but as soon as he recognized Fletcher, he dismissed them, saying "You must excuse me now, gentlemen, I have an appointment with Colonel Fletcher and his friends." Fletcher spoke to Grant about Josephine and her family. He noted President Lincoln's admiration for Henry Clay and his long-standing support for the Union. Acting out of respect for Josephine, her daughter Lula, and the unborn child, Grant wrote out two travel passes including free Federal transport. One pass allowed Josephine and her daughter to proceed to St. Louis; another authorized Hickman to accompany them as far as Cairo, Illinois, requiring that he return to Vicksburg on the first steamship to await parole.

Turning to Hickman, Grant asked: "Has Mrs. Erwin any money?" "None that will pass in the North," was the reply. "Then give her this," he said, handing Hickman a $50 greenback. When

Fig. 5.7 Josephine R. Erwin

5.8 Gen. Ulysses S. Grant, 1863.
Library of Congress

Grant extended his hand to Josephine as she was leaving, she refused to shake it. She could not shake the hand of the man she felt was responsible for her husband's death.[18]

The following morning, Josephine, Lula, and Hickman left Vicksburg for St. Louis. Although subject to Grant's limitation on carrying possessions, Josephine sewed the Sixth Missouri battle flag inside her petticoat. The party traveled on the steamship *Imperial*, and the officer on board, Custis Washington, wrote to Josephine "not to hesitate to call on me for anything that may add to your comfort or convenience. I trust your state room is as comfortable as possible."[19]

When Josephine arrived in Independence, she found that her mother and two daughters had moved to another residence in the city. The Jones Hotel had been converted to a hospital for soldiers wounded in numerous battles near Independence.

The town was divided between Union and Confederate sympathizers. During the summer of 1863, seventeen young women in Independence were charged with aiding and abetting a rebel outlaw gang. Union officers claimed that the women spied on Federal forces and arranged to buy ammunition for a band of Confederate volunteers under the command of William Quantrill. The women were arrested and placed in a three-story brick building used as a jail in Kansas City. "After a few days, the building began shaking and a guard shouted 'the guardhouse is falling,' and he hadn't more than gotten the words out of his mouth when there was a crash and the women prisoners were buried under the brick and mortar of the old building." Four women were killed and seven wounded. Confederate supporters believed that Union troops had purposefully destroyed the building and called for vengeance.[20]

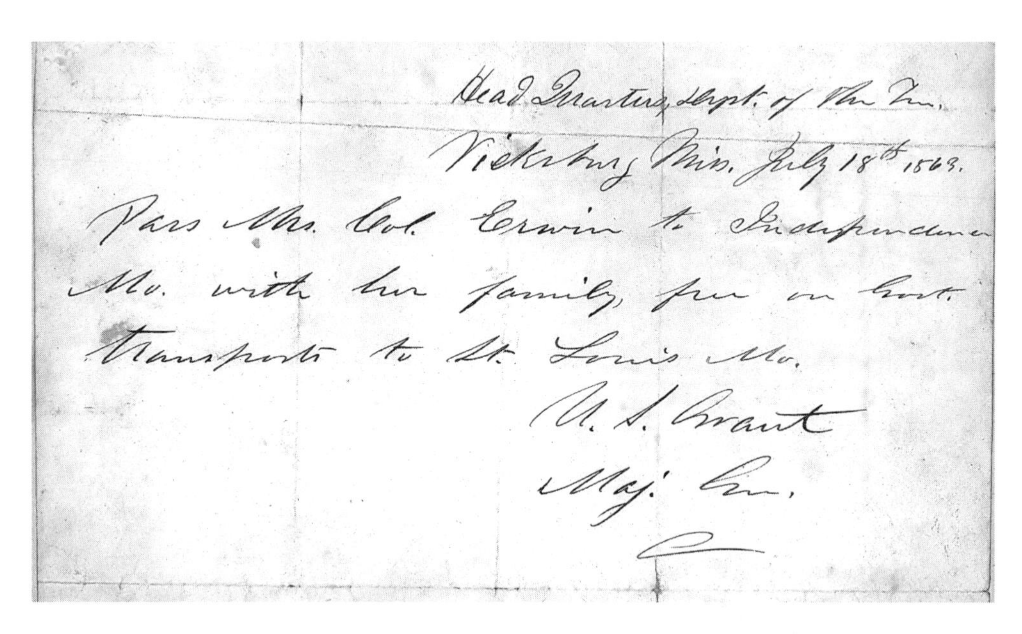

Head Quarters, Dept. of the Tenn.
Vicksburg Miss. July 18th 1863.
Pass Mrs. Col. Erwin to Independence
Mo. with her family, free on Govt.
transports to St. Louis Mo.
U. S. Grant
Maj. Gen.

Fig. 5.9 Pass to Independence, Missouri, for "Mrs. Col. Erwin" Signed by General Grant. *UK*

Quantrill's volunteers, which included several men that later became well known outlaws after the war, Frank James, Jesse James, and Cole Younger, were enraged by the deaths of the girls. On August 21, they sacked Lawrence, Kansas, burning every house in the town and killing 150 men and boys. In response, the Federal commander, Brig. Gen. Thomas Ewing, signed General Order No. 11 effective August 25, 1863, requiring all persons living in three counties including Jackson, an area one hundred miles long and thirty miles wide including 20,000 people, to evacuate their homes within fifteen days and be interviewed at the nearest military post about their loyalties. Any man or woman judged to be a Confederate sympathizer was fined and jailed. To avoid prison, each person was required to take an oath of loyalty to the satisfaction of the commanding officer and obtain a certificate permitting them to move from their home to a protected district. Both Union and Confederate families tried to follow the order, traveling along roads to a military post or camping on the rivers in the area seeking transport. Outlaw gangs robbed and killed many hundreds of people.[21] Josephine obtained an order of protection from the Federal Commander in St. Louis that exempted her from General Order No. 11. This allowed her family to live in relative safety. Maj. Gen. John M. Schofield, who must have been aware of her meeting with General Grant, ordered that "All officers and soldiers in the service of the United States or the State of Ms. [Missouri] are hereby required to give protection to the person and property of Mrs. Josephine Erwin and to permit her to live in peace at her home in Independence."[22]

Josephine Erwin was appointed the executrix of her husband's estate, which consisted of his Confederate army payment to widows (which had no value in Missouri) and his real estate. Her husband's farm property and land in Independence may have provided a small income.

She devoted herself to Eugene's estate and began to establish a closer relationship with the Clay family. She wrote her former husband's uncle, John M. Clay, during the Christmas period of 1863 and received a letter back from him in early January 1864.

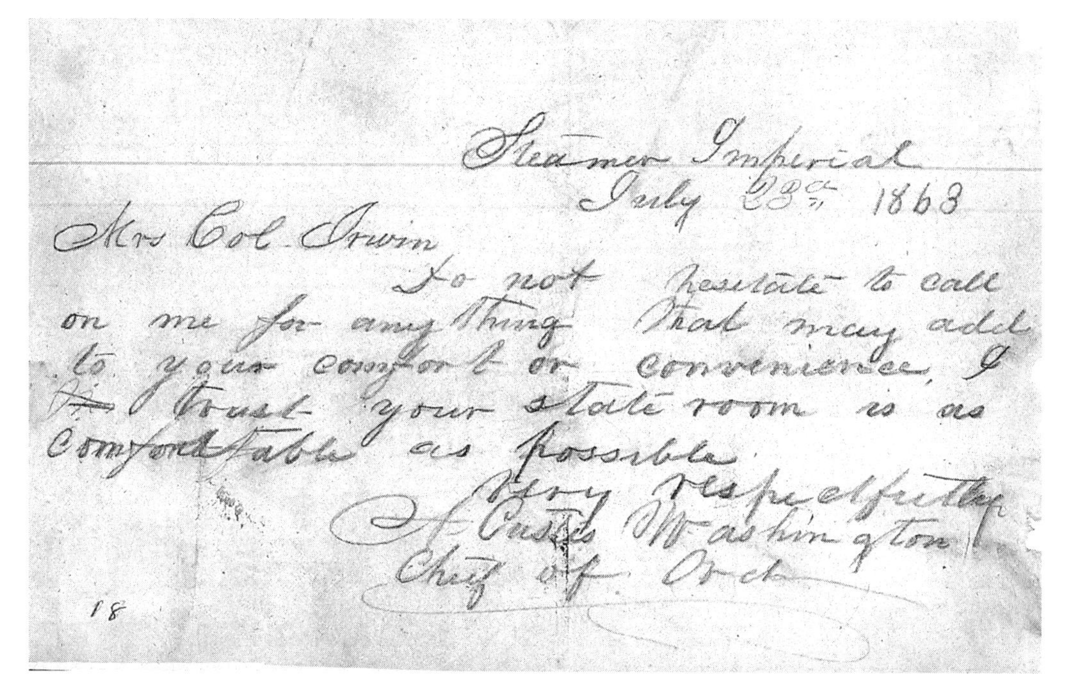

Steamer Imperial
July 23rd 1863
Mrs Col Irwin
Do not hesitate to call on me for any thing that may add to your comfort or convenience, I trust your state room is as comfortable as possible
Very respectfully
A Custis Washington
Chief of Ord

18

Fig. 5.10 Note from Custis Washington, Chief of Steamer *Imperial,* July 23, 1863. *UK*

27th Dec 1863

Dear Josephine,

I received yesterday your favor of the 20th and regret that you should have been so slow in writing to me. We have heard nothing of you since your letter in October. This cruel war has brought great distress and suffering to the whole country, and although yours have not been the least, still you ought not to forget that you have sacred duties to perform toward your little children, nor abandon yourself to grief and despair.

Our family has suffered much in this war. Besides Eugene, Henry Clay (III) has died in it and many of our relations are still engaged in fighting on both sides, and others have lost all their property and been exiled from their homes. My brother James and his family are now in Montreal and we are expecting to hear of his death every day, his physicians having told him he cannot live. His disease is consumption brought on by exposure incident to the War. I went to see him last month. His wife though extremely distressed about his condition takes great comfort and consolation in the assurance that he will die a Christian death, and that her loss will be his gain.[23]

My mother's health is better than when I last wrote you, in fact than it has been for a year, but she is of course very feeble, nearly 83 years old.

My brother Thomas is US minister at Honduras has been gone a year and his family have rented and are living at Ashland.

[a section was cut out of the letter]

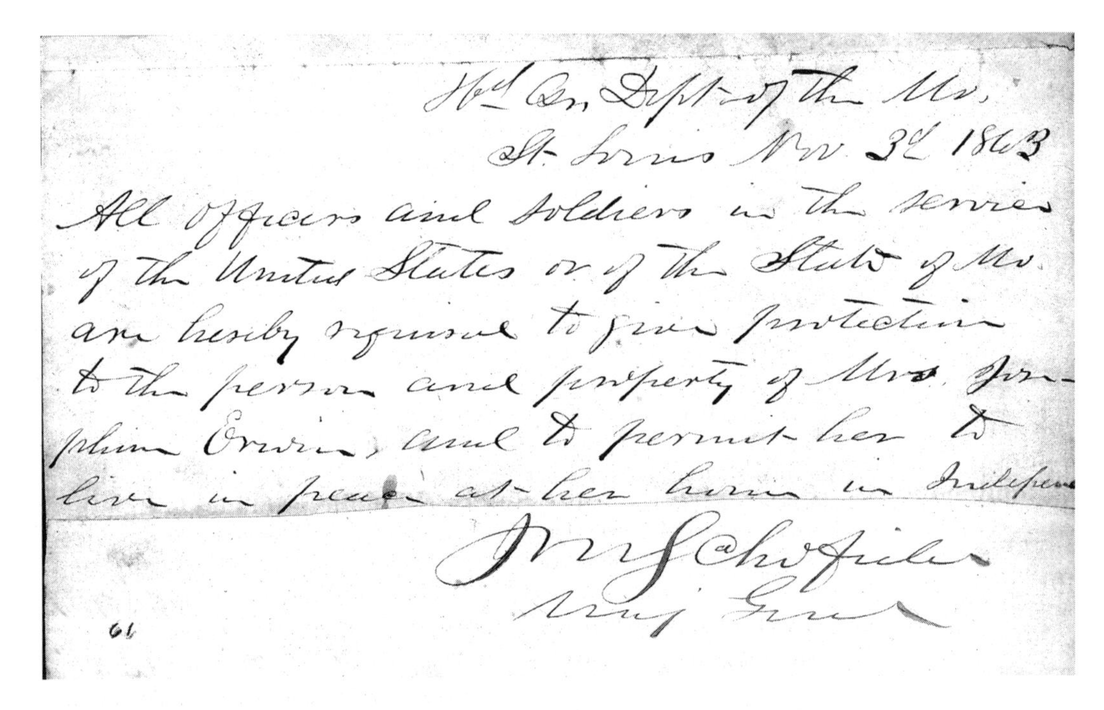
Hd Qrs, Dept of the Mo.
St. Louis Nov 3d 1863
All officers and soldiers in the service of the United States or of the State of Mo. are hereby requested to give protection to the person and property of Mrs. Josephine Erwin, and to permit her to live in peace at her home in Independ
J M Schofield
Maj Genl
61

Fig. 5.11 Order of Protection from Maj. Gen. John M. Schofield, November 3, 1863. *UK*

> You will soon be relieved of such vexation. But by all means do not dispair, remember your duties as a Christian woman. I trust your health may soon be restored to you. My mother sends love to you and the children. I enclose a Christmas present from her. Please do write frequently.
>
> Yours affectionately, John M. Clay[24]

On January 26, 1864, Josephine gave birth to her fourth daughter, named Eugenia in honor of her late husband. The child lived only a few days. This was a low point in her life. Her husband's death and the loss of her baby daughter transformed the bright personality that had charmed her father's guests into a serious and single-minded young woman dedicated to the survival of her family in wartime Missouri.

Josephine's terrible experience in the Civil War changed her life, and the war began a change in the role of women in American society. She was empowered, as were many women, to live a more independent life. She later wrote that she was determined to "paddle my own canoe."[25]

Mrs. Lucretia Clay and her son John reiterated their invitation to Josephine to visit Lexington. They wanted to provide a safer place for the Erwin family to live during the war.[26] But Josephine may have considered the risk of traveling with a large family during wartime too great. She did not make the trip to Lexington until the war ended two years later.

Part III

Josephine Clay, Horsewoman of the Bluegrass

Chapter 6

John M. Clay

Soft winds belong to that era most blest,
When springtime harbored not tears.[1]

John Morrison Clay, the youngest child of Henry and Lucretia Clay, was born in 1821. He was probably named for his grandfather, the Rev. John Clay, and Col. James Morrison, Henry Clay's friend and a major benefactor of Transylvania College. At age thirteen, John attended Edgehill Seminary in Princeton, New Jersey, where he had a reputation for being rebellious and undisciplined. On one occasion, he broke the rules and was required to address the entire student body with an apology. His father wrote a letter to the headmaster, Enoch Wines, saying that a private apology "ought to be deemed sufficient . . . that a public apology would exhibit [his son] in a mortifying attitude, which would wound intensely the sensibility of any boy and might have a permanent injurious operation upon his future life."[2]

John Clay eventually adjusted to the school and graduated. Headmaster Wines wrote to Henry Clay to say that the young man had "fine capabilities, excellent principles, great independence & strength, a nice sense of honor . . . he lacks only religion . . . ."[3] After graduation, he attended the Princeton College of Law. Following a bout with typhoid fever in the summer of 1836, he did not return to Princeton, but attended Transylvania College. The following year he returned to Princeton, but after a short time left without graduating to take courses at a college in Pennsylvania before returning to live at Ashland.[4]

In 1841, John Clay joined his father when he returned to Washington, describing the trip in a letter to his mother.

Brown's Indian Queen Hotel, Washington
May 24th 1841

My dear Mother,

We arrived here yesterday evening after a rapid and very comfortable journey. We met with an accident on the railroad between Frederick & Baltimore which but for good fortune would have proved calamitous in the extreme. As the train of cars turned a very short curve when the road winds round the base of a hill with a precipice abruptly commencing within a few feet of the rails, the loco-motive encountered a bull, upset him and without running over him with the wheels, dropped him immediately under the passenger cars, all of which ran over & crushed him; and we were thrown with violent shock off the rails, had the loco-motive been thrown off, we should all have gone down a steep descent of 50 yards; as it was, however, with the exception of 2 hours detention, we suffered no injury or inconvenience. Having arrived at this place in time for a nights rest Papa seems entirely refreshed from the fatigues of the journey and desires me to say to you that although still complaining, he hopes & expects his health to improve. . . . Members of Congress are flocking into the city and no doubt on Monday next a sufficient number will be present to constitute a quorum. I will not detain you longer with a detail of the rumors & reports various in character which are in circulation & so hoping this will find you & all at home well. I remain dear mother,

Your aff. son

J. M. Clay

P. S. We are to board at Mrs Bowen's on C Street back of Gadsby's Hotel[5]

Fig. 6.1 John M. Clay

John Clay was expected to follow his father's career as a lawyer, but his introverted personality was not suited for public life. A photographic portrait of him shows a slender man with a thin goatee, dressed in a fine waistcoat and tie. His gaze is pensive, focused in the distance. The Clay family was alarmed by John's drinking and periods of depression. In April 1845, when he was twenty-four years old, he was hospitalized at the Kentucky Lunatic Asylum. He was found wandering in the woods at 2 a. m. threatening to commit suicide after being rejected by a lady friend.[6] His parents were worried. Their oldest son, Theodore, was committed permanently at the same institution after a serious head injury. When John was released, his father encouraged him to work at Ashland. Given responsibility for the stock operation, he demonstrated both industry and talent for breeding and racing Thoroughbred horses.

In 1845, Henry Clay received three Thoroughbred horses as gifts from political admirers that would become the foundation for the future success of the farm. The broodmares *Margaret Wood* and *Magnolia* were obtained from Col. Wade Hampton of South Carolina and Dr. William Mercer of New Orleans, and Commodore Charles Morgan of South Carolina presented Clay with the imported stallion *Yorkshire*. These horses produced a long line of successful racers. Descendants of the two broodmares included eleven future winners of the Kentucky Derby.[7]

When the progeny of *Yorkshire* was offered for sale, Clay proclaimed: "Gentlemen, with this great promise of the equine family before you, there is every chance of success. If you will take into consideration that your enterprise [may be] greater than your bank accounts, and never underrate your enemy, you are bound to succeed."[8] *Yorkshire* became one of the great sires of America, and the breeding success of Ashland and other central Kentucky horse farms was instrumental in the development of central Kentucky as a center for Thoroughbred horses. The beautiful rolling countryside and rich, limestone soil in the Lexington area was well suited for horse farms.

In addition to Ashland, other prominent horse farms established in central Kentucky at this time included Woodburn Farm, comprised of four thousand acres under the management of A. J. Alexander; Elmendorf Stud Farm, founded by Milton H. Sanford with five hundred acres; and Runnymede Stud, owned by the partnership of Catesby Woodford and Col. Ezekiel Clay, a distant cousin of Henry Clay, with five hundred acres.[9]

When his father died in 1852, John Clay was willed two hundred acres to be used for the continuation of Ashland Stock Farm, including Thoroughbred horses, cattle, sheep, and other pedigree stock originally purchased by Henry Clay. John received a half interest in the most valuable horses. His mother inherited the other half, and as soon as the estate was settled, she made a gift of her share to her son.[10]

In August 1853, John Clay borrowed against the two hundred acres he inherited to build a new home on the property called "Ashland on Tates Creek Pike."[11] Maj. Thomas Lewinski, an architect from England who had moved to Lexington and married a Clay cousin, Mary Louisa Watkins, was commissioned to design the house on the highest point of land on his farm.[12] It was located less than a quarter-mile and in full view of the Ashland mansion to the northeast. John Clay invited his mother and her house servants to move to the new home at the time the old Ashland mansion, inherited by his brother James, was being rebuilt.[13] Lucretia Clay lived with her son at Ashland on Tates Creek Pike until she died twelve years later.[14]

John Clay's new house was a two-story, brick farmhouse with a metal roof, a large front porch, and a brick patio that runs around the house. The main front porch faced the town of Lexington to the north-west. It was said that both the nearby Ashland mansion and the monument to Henry Clay at the Lexington Cemetery several miles away could be seen from the front porch. Inside the door was a spiral staircase to the second floor. There were six bedrooms on the second floor, of which three were part of a servants' wing which used a kitchen staircase. The first floor had twelve-foot ceilings and included a parlor, dining room, and kitchen. The main gate to the farm was on the Tates Creek Pike with a gravel road curving up the hill to the house.[15]

Fig. 6.2 Star Davis at Ashland Stock Farm by Thomas J. Scott, 1856

John Clay continued his father's racing establishment using similar light blue colors and added a coiled snake on the cap with the motto, "Don't tread on me."[16] *An Historical Account of Racing in the United States* edited by Lyman H. Weeks, describes how John M. Clay used the mares he inherited to become "one of the most successful breeders in nineteenth century America."[17] He became famous for successfully breeding his mares to a small number of stallions including *Yorkshire*, the imported *Glencoe*, and the famous racer *Lexington* at A. J. Alexander's Woodburn Farm.

Magnolia, a horse that never raced, was sent to Woodburn to be bred to *Lexington*. On April 18, 1856, Clay wrote in the Ashland Stock Book that "*Magnolia* had a bay colt by *Lexington* called by me this day *Kentucky*." For unknown reasons, the name of the horse was later changed to *Daniel Boone*. In 1861, *Magnolia* was again bred to *Lexington*, and Clay again named a foal *Kentucky*. Clay brought the large and rangy bay colt as a two-year-old to the Paterson, New Jersey autumn meeting where *Kentucky* won a mile sweepstakes, beating *Minnie Minor*. After the race, John R. Purdy bought *Kentucky* and another horse for $6,000, a famously low price. After being beaten in the Jersey Derby by *Norfolk* the following year, *Kentucky* won twenty-two straight races and was completely in a class by himself, one of three racehorses that dominated an era of racing.[18] The other two, *Asteroid* and *Norfolk*, were also offspring of *Lexington*.

Henry Clay's first stallion investment, *Buzzard*, purchased in 1806 in a five-man syndicate, was the grandsire of the stallion *Glencoe*, standing at stud on the farm of William Frank Harper.[19] John Clay often bred his mares to *Glencoe*, and when he sent *Margaret Woods* to Harper's farm, the result was a new foal he named *Star Davis*. By 1856, *Star Davis* had become one of Ashland's most successful racers, and Clay wanted to honor the horse that he hoped would be successful at stud. He commissioned a painting by a new artist, Thomas J. Scott.

Fig. 6.3 Pedigree Wheel for Star Davis

Scott was born in Pennsylvania, and after being educated in medicine and pharmacy, migrated in 1855 to Kentucky where he developed a fondness for painting horses. He became a pupil of the famous horse painter Edward Troye and showed a talent for obtaining good likenesses by using his knowledge of anatomy. *Star Davis* was one of his first commissions.[20] The large horse dominates Scott's painting with a background scene at Ashland showing a Latting Observatory near John Clay's private race track, the first one-mile training course in Kentucky.[21]

John Clay kept detailed pedigree records for his horses, and for *Star Davis* he created a pedigree wheel that could be shown to the owners of prospective broodmares. For the next twenty years, *Star Davis* sired successful Thoroughbreds at Ashland, and when nearing retirement, became national news as the sire of *Day Star*, the 1878 winner of the Kentucky Derby, the first Derby winner bred at Ashland.

Magnolia, known as "the Empress of the Stud Book," produced great race horse descendants that numbered in the hundreds. *Magnolia* died after giving birth to *Victory* by *Uncle Vic*, a son of *Lexington*, at 6:30 a.m. on March 29, 1864.[22] *Victory* first raced as a three-year-old in the 1867 Phoenix Stakes in Lexington finishing 4, 1, 3, and 2 in four one-mile heats. Over the next five years, *Victory* started seventeen times accumulating seven wins. In 1873, Gen. George Custer purchased *Victory* and shortened the name. *Vic* was the horse he used at the Battle of the Little Big Horn three years later.[23]

Ashland's Stock Book reported in 1860 that "*Magnolia* had a sorrel filly, [with a] white face the 6th of February by *Yorkshire*." The foal was named *Skedaddle* and showed exceptional speed in winning a race program in St. Louis. Unfortunately, the racer was injured and was retired to stud at Ashland.

Racing, as with all pastimes, was interrupted by the Civil War. When hostilities began, Lexington had grown to a town of 9,000, but the outskirts of the town near Ashland had not been developed and looked very much as it had when Josephine Russell visited the town as a child in 1843. While the outward appearance was the same, intense fighting between Confederate and Federal supporters was taking place near Ashland. The Clay family was divided with Henry Clay's son James acting as a spokesman and prominent supporter of the South, while his brothers Thomas and John backed the Union.

Josephine Clay wrote:

> Kentucky, as one of the Border States, was unwilling for her lovely blue grass pastures to become blood-drenched battle-fields, declared neutrality—armed if necessary. Her protests were unheeded, military camps soon were making their appearance and . . . the country was amazed and shocked by the outrages perpetrated by bands of "Irregular Troops," as they called themselves, and claiming allegiance to the Southern Confederacy . . . .[24]

This was a difficult period for John Clay and other owners of horse farms. There was a constant threat that horses would be commandeered by the soldiers of both sides of the conflict. Many farms shipped their horses to the safety of northern farms, but John Clay continued breeding operations. The Ashland Stock Book lists five foals in 1861, seven in 1862, eleven in 1863, and six in 1864. In 1863, John Clay mortgaged four horses to support a $1,000 loan from the Bank of Kentucky.[25]

On June 9, 1864, Gen. John Hunt Morgan's Confederate Raiders staged a daring raid on Lexington, setting a series of fires at military warehouses and the railway depot. While Federal troops were putting out the fires, Morgan led a column into the center of Lexington, capturing the Federal battery, and camping near Ashland.

The following morning, Morgan's scouts raided Ashland, capturing several Thoroughbreds, including *Skedaddle.* General Morgan gathered the new horse herd at the rear of his column and marched to a camp near Georgetown, fifteen miles away.

Clay rode his fastest horse in pursuit of Morgan's column. When he reached the camp, he confronted Morgan and demanded the return of his horses. Morgan responded, "I will not dismount any one of my men for a Union man, but if you want to buy your horses back, go ahead."[26] Clay made this entry in his Daily Journal for June 10:

> I rose at 4:40 and while reading the Bible and prayers was summoned to the stable by Bill telling me the rebels were carrying off my horses. They went with Sked, Tara, G. Wood, and Apollo. About 9:00 I followed them to Georgetown and succeeded in getting them back by paying $900. Stayed all night at Pratts Tavern in Georgetown after great anxiety and trouble about getting the horses from the Rebel robbers.[27]

Magnolia was the dam of *Madeline,* listed as a broodmare for the first time in the Ashland Stock Book in 1862. After four years of unsuccessful breeding or foals that did not survive, *Madeline* was bred to the imported stallion *Australian* (GB) in 1867 and produced a live foal that Clay named

Magpie. The foal was jointly owned by John Clay and the estate of his brother, James B. Clay, who died in Canada during the Civil War. Two years later, in May 1869, John Clay sold *Madeline* and his share of *Magpie* to his nephew, Capt. James (Jimmy) B. Clay, Jr.[28]

Captain Clay became acquainted with the much-admired daughter of U. S. Senator James Burnie Beck from Lexington. He wanted to marry Margaret (Maggie) B. Beck. Although Senator Beck had been a friend and supporter of Henry Clay, he did not approve of the match, probably because Jimmy Clay returned from four years of combat experience in the Confederate Army with a drinking problem. In 1870, Maggie Beck married James K. Corcoran, an heir of the wealthy Corcoran banking family in Washington, D. C., but she died soon after her marriage. As a tribute, despite the "pangs of despised love," Captain Clay renamed his new mare *Maggie B. B.*[29]

Maggie B. B. was an example of John Clay's breeding prowess, with success coming after he sold the horse. *Maggie B. B.* became one of the most famous broodmares in Thoroughbred racing, the dam of the winner of two Triple Crown races and two classic races in Europe. *Maggie B. B.* produced a chestnut colt *Harold,* the winner of the Preakness in 1879; a chestnut colt *Panique*, the winner of the Belmont in 1884; and a brown colt *Iroquois*, the first American-bred winner of the Epsom Derby and the St. Leger Stakes in 1881.[30] The trading of shares on Wall Street was halted when the victory of *Iroquois* was announced on the ticker.[31]

John Clay's breeding success was drawing national interest in his stock farm. A journalist from a turf newspaper, *Wilkes Spirit of the Times*, visited his farm and filed the following report:

> I availed myself of fortunate circumstances to pay a visit to the farm of John M. Clay, Esq., Kentucky's foremost breeder of the race-horse—I say foremost, because while the Alexanders and Keene Richards, and possibly others, are engaged in breeding on a larger scale, I think he is entitled to precedence in time and pre-eminence in the production of celebrated winners.
>
> A delightful walk of about two miles from the ancient Phoenix [Hotel], which is renewing itself in grander proportions, brought me all aglow in the bracing air of this crisp November morning, to the hospitable door of Mr. Clay's mansion. It is a fine brick residence, situated upon an eminence on a part of the estate of his father, Henry Clay .... The whole estate is overlooked from the house and is divided into fields of convenient size, whether for tillage or pasture; and the *coup d'oeil*—taking in the distant stable, sheds and fences [about one hundred yards east of the house]; the private course [about twenty yards west from the house], with the Latting Observatory in the centre; and the grand parks of venerable ash, denuded of their foliage, but relieved by thick bushes of mistletoe, carpeted with the evergreen blue grass, and dotted here and there by illustrious scions of the Thoroughbred, or magnificent specimens of short-horn, gamboling in the warm sunlight on the slopes, or grazing contently in the rich intervals—was most charming ....
>
> The warm greeting over, we were introduced to T. B Paterson, Esq. [John M. Clay's trainer] ...on a visit to the home of *Magnolia*, mother not of "dead empires, but of living prodigies." We soon formed a procession ... to the somewhat solitary quarters of *Star Davis*, one of Mr. Clay's specialties—a magnate whose name is familiar to breeder and turfites from Maine to California.
>
> "Ho! Harve! [former slave and longtime Clay employee]. What's that horse doing with the

> bar there!" suddenly exclaimed Mr. Clay. Turning from *Star Davis* his eye caught the figure of a three year old bay stallion pulling with his teeth at a single board, separating him from a half dozen yearlings of various sexes in the adjoining paddock. "Practicing at the bar, I reckon, with a sly wink at me," said Paterson, sotto voce. Hastening to the scene, we arrive in time to prevent mischief and to discover that *Magnolia's* last production from *Lexington*, full brother to *Kentucky*, was inspecting the fence which separated him from closer companionship, and had got down two-thirds of the bars between them.
>
> In the tempting lot adjoining were *Magnolia's* last—a sorrel filly by *Uncle Vic*, a young horse [*Victory*]. *Mag* having missed to *Lexington* the year before, *Ballon* was substituted for his embrace. This yearling filly is remarkably promising . . . .
>
> But what great, big splendidly got up mare is this approaching? Have you ever heard of the slashing race at St. Louis, mile heats, three in five, won by *Skedaddle* in 1864? Well, here she is—the mother of winners no less renowned then *Kentucky*, and I trust no less numerous than her great dam *Magnolia*. She was captured by the rebels, pursued, overtaken and ransomed by Mr. Clay at Georgetown. Accident having incapacitated her for the turf, she is consigned to the breeding paddock.
>
> The next field was honored by the presence of only two equine celebrities; but they were venerable for their age, valuable for their produce and historic in their relations to the soil they trod. Both have been blind these many years, and are probably past the capacity to breed, albeit their coats are as sleek as three years old, and one of them has a suckling by her side. *Margaret Woods* and *Heraldry*, both gifts with imp. *Yorkshire*, from enthusiastic friends to Henry Clay . . . . Who can estimate the value of *Yorkshire* to the racing excellence of the American Turf?
>
> Of John Clay's personal peculiarities it may not become me to speak here. Whatever his faults, I am sure they arise from the over impulsiveness of a high nervous organization. [He appeared quite eccentric to many people because he was brutally honest in commenting about horses and people. While horse buyers were always interested in hearing about the deficiencies of his horses, comments about rival horses and their owners led to many disputes].
>
> He is generous, chivalrous and honorable to the last degree, it were superfluous in me to avouch. But I may with propriety speak of his unswerving loyalty to his country . . . .[32]

Clay's daily journal describes the long illness of his mother Lucretia, who died on April 7, 1864. He now lived alone at Ashland on Tates Creek Pike with his servants. Under the terms of Henry Clay's will, Eugene Erwin's children were to receive a one-fourth interest in $7,500 after his widow's death. John M. Clay wrote Josephine Erwin on August 25, 1864 to say: "I am glad you are pleased with my suggestions in reference to the legacy of the little children. I will do the best I can in the matter and will report progress to you . . . . I am your affectionate Uncle, John M. Clay. P.S. Do let us continue to correspond frequently."[33]

Josephine Erwin decided that she would bring her family to Lexington to receive the inheritance for her children and stay for a period with the Clay family. It is likely that she did not plan to stay more than a year. On August 30, 1865, she purchased at auction for $700 several lots including a forty-acre pasture and an area called "Erwin's addition to the city of Independence."[34] On November 14, she rented these properties for a period of one year.[35]

The date of her arrival in Lexington, November 23, 1865, was documented in John Clay's daily journal. "Mrs. Erwin, Mother and children arrived tonight." On the following Sunday, he "attended church in the evening and talked with Mrs. Erwin and Mother." References in the journal indicate that Josephine and her family were living with Susan Jacob Clay, the widow of James Clay, in the Ashland mansion.

On February 15, 1866 the Ashland estate was sold at auction to Kentucky A & M College, and Josephine Erwin, her mother, and three daughters probably moved to Ashland on Tates Creek Pike at that time. On March 9, John's daily journal mentions that Josephine "fixed about ¼ acre in old garden," and on April 5, "Mrs. Erwin planted carrots, parsnips, radishes, and onions in the garden."[36] On June 8, John wrote a letter to "My Dear Niece" from Paterson, New Jersey, thanking Josephine for having his bedroom renovated and declaring that:

> I wish I could always do my "level best" as you have the habit of doing. My motto is "prodesse quam conspici"—be, rather than seem . . . . If you have retired from the Turf, since Joe Davis was sold [Josephine probably objected to the sale], I hope you won't think of leaving your home till I return. I call it your home, because I want you so to think it, and although my home, it would be a poor desolate home without you. I was offered $15,000 for Gilroy last night. My price is $25,000.

He planned to return after the Saratoga races on July 1, 1866.

Some people in Lexington who followed Clay family activities were disturbed about Josephine's decision to move into John Clay's home. They believed it improper for a thirty-year-old widow and her family to live and work in the home of a forty-three-year-old bachelor.[37]

On July 4, three days after John Clay returned from Saratoga, New York, he made the following entry: "Saw my future wife, God bless her." The following evening "at night conversed lovingly with Jo and returned at 11:45" (indicating that she was living elsewhere when he returned). On July 7, he wrote about his marriage as he would have described a routine event on the farm:

> I rose at 4:30. Breakfast at 7:00. Bill assisted me in grinding some meal. Obtained a marriage license by friendly assistance of B.F. Pettit. Jo and I were married by Mr. Brank at 8:20 p.m. at Pettits. Brank & us all that were present. We returned home at 9:30. Cloudy warm some little rain at night.[38]

Josephine had married a grandson, and now a son of Henry Clay. Although they did not invite family and friends to celebrate their wedding, they organized a "Paper Wedding" at their home on Monday evening, July 8, 1867 to celebrate their first wedding anniversary.[39]

Josephine wanted to change John's lifestyle. During the winter months, his custom was to spend the day at his club on North Broadway, gamble at whist, and drink until late in the evening. Often, he described himself as too sick and drunk to return home until the following day. Before his marriage, on Christmas Day 1865: he "attended church, drank wine and got in a row on Cheapside [the market square in Lexington]."[40] The day after their wedding, July 8, 1866, John and Josephine "formed some good resolutions about business and pleasure and put our trust in the Powers Above."[41] From that date forward, there is no reference to drinking at home in his daily journal.

However, when Clay traveled with his horses to race tracks, he reported in his letters to Josephine that he was often sick from too much drink. Although none of Josephine's letters to her husband have survived, it is apparent from Clay's responses that she often wrote letters criticizing his lifestyle when he was away.[42]

In 1867, Clay was told by Rev. Dr. Jacob Shipman that he should not enter Christ Episcopal Church because he was running horses. He answered at once, saying: "Why, doctor, there's Bill Bradley, he trots horses. Why can't a man run into heaven as well as trot." The congregation thought John's response amusing, and the Lexington newspapers reported the incident and said there would be very few members of Christ Church if Dr. Shipman's standard were applied to others in the congregation. From that time on, John only occasionally visited Christ Church but regularly attended Catholic mass with Josephine.[43]

Perhaps this incident encouraged Josephine Clay to write stories about the clergy and racing. "Why There Was No Sermon at Mount Gilead" tells the story of a minister who substitutes as a jockey and wins a race for a member of his parish. It begins:

When God erects a house of prayer,
The Devil always builds a chapel there,
And t'will be found on examination,
The latter has the largest congregation.[44]

Josephine had experience in riding and caring for horses at her family's farm in Missouri and became John's partner in the management of the horses and other livestock at Ashland. According to Clay's diary, John and Josephine arose daily between 4:30 and 5 a.m. and, after feeding the horses and caring for injuries, read the bible and had prayers before breakfast.[45] The horses were kept out in the fields in open sheds with a southern exposure, rather than in barns with stalls, and were given plenty of hay and corn. Much care was required in storms to avoid injury to the animals.

John Clay often participated in private races arranged at the Ashland training track. In her story "Honors Are Easy," Josephine describes how owners with differences of opinion about the speed of their horses offered the ultimatum: "put up or shut up." John Clay sometimes made bets totaling as much as five or ten thousand dollars—half forfeit. The forfeit money was deposited by each gentleman, and if the horse did not run, the forfeit was paid to the other owner.[46]

Josephine's story "Who Rode La Sylphide?" tells the story of a newly married horse owner who bets more than he can afford on his own horse. When the jockey is injured by a runaway horse just before the race, a mysterious new jockey appears that can not be identified by local punters due to a heavy scarf. Is the jockey the owner's new wife? Josephine told her grandchildren that she had ridden and won a private match race for her husband.[47]

John Clay wanted to commission a painting of *Skedaddle,* the horse that he retrieved from Gen. John Hunt Morgan's raiders in the Civil War. Thomas J. Scott returned in 1869, to paint *Skedaddle* with a new foal, *Squeeze'em.* The view in the background includes the farm's main pasture and Clay's home, Ashland on Tates Creek Pike.

For the next generation, *Skedaddle* was Ashland's most successful broodmare. When *Skedaddle* died in 1889, the *New York Times* published the following note: "*Skedaddle*, 29 years old, a well-known brood mare belonging to Mrs. John M. Clay, has died of old age. She was by imp. *Yorkshire,* dam *Magnolia*, by imp. *Glencoe*. From her have descended some of the most famous performers that ever graced the American turf, such as *Kaloolah, Day Star, Leveller, La Sylphide, Sachem,* and *Saranac*."[48]

Fig. 6.4 Skedaddle and Squeeze'em by Thomas J. Scott, 1869

Squeeze'em was bred to *Star Davis* and produced *Day Star,* Ashland's first winner of the Kentucky Derby.[49]

While John traveled to racetracks throughout the East, often acting as owner, trainer, and stable hand for his horses, Josephine managed the farm and was in correspondence with her husband about the care of the horses and the operation of the farm. Each morning, Uncle Harve, the long-standing stable hand, would meet with Josephine to discuss the farm operation. Lula, reported the following conversation: "Have you fed the broodmares this morning, Harve?" "Oh yes, Miss Josie." "What did you give them?" "Quart and a half of hominy, two quarts oats, arm full of hay .... I must go and feed them mares right now." Lula credited Uncle Harve for the outstanding conditioning of the horses.[50]

Lula told several stories about Uncle Harve:

> After he was freed under the terms of Henry Clay's Will, Uncle Harve continued to work for wages at Ashland. His interest in the Thoroughbreds he cared for was great, and he never failed to attend a race meeting when "one of ours" was to start. To witness first under the wire, the colors buff and blue, was a great joy, and he always celebrated the victory. But a day came when he arrived home to Ashland just after a race in a state of excitement. "Waterloo, he win de race, but the next horse's owner claimed a foul—and Mars John Clay say "if Waterloo is ruled off, men will fall like shelled corn. I know that family, and they can shoot, so I left."
>
> One long remembered day, Uncle Harve burst in to see the family. "A bear, Marse John, a bear" he cried " bear's raring up on his hind legs walkin round dem mares and foals just like folks." This incredible story was true. A bear was having the time of his life with the Thoroughbreds.[51] [The old Ashland mansion had been purchased by Kentucky A & M College which used it as a residence for it's regent and a museum including a small zoo.]
>
> Uncle Harve loved the time he was passing the drawing room window at Ashland, and he saw a dark man drinking wine with Marse Henry Clay, and soon there gathered outside

FFig. 6.5 Racing Purses Won by Ashland Stock Farm

> the window an excited circle of dark faces. It was the President of Liberia, who made a pilgrimage to Ashland to express the gratitude of his people for Clay's support for the new nation. Clay explained to his guest that on principle, as an evil in itself, he was opposed to slavery which in time would threaten the existence of the Union.[52]

Josephine carefully saved the colorful silk purses brought back by her husband after his horses won stakes races. The purses, filled with coins and hung on a wire over the track, were given to the owner of the winning horse. She was able to preserve the fabrics of five purses which were later framed under glass.[53]

In honor of her husband's fiftieth birthday, Josephine Clay wrote a dramatic play, *The Three Wise Women of Boston*, which was performed "by his children" at the mansion at Ashland on February 21, 1871. The play has been lost, but the playbill lists her daughters as the dramatis personae: Lucretia, Nettie, and Mary. Each was to make a congratulatory address in the finale. This was the first of several, large-scale receptions with drama and music that Josephine organized for friends and family.[54]

When John M. Clay traveled with his horses, he wrote letters to his wife from the tracks including Buckeye (Cincinnati, Ohio), Chickasaw (Memphis, Tennessee), Jerome Park (New York), Laclede (St. Louis, Missouri), Long Branch (New Jersey), Monmouth Park (New Jersey), Nashville (Tennessee), Saratoga (New York), and Woodlawn (Louisville, Kentucky).

John Clay was among the horse owners who rarely expected to win, so when a horse did perform well, he was always surprised. His letters to Josephine often contained this personal drama at the track.

Woodlawn 1 p.m. 7th Oct [ca. 1869]

My Dear Wife,

Sally got lamer after the race, is excited & her pulse 46 to 51 ever since. She is running today . . . 3 best in 5. If she were all right it would be a hard race for her to win, but as she is, her chances are desperate. I shall try not to abuse her if she can't win. I am plenty tired of this place & plenty sorry I came to it. I may stay to see the race tomorrow and if I do not come home till Sunday will write tomorrow [in the] afternoon mail. Not a word from home yet. Hope for the best. We will cut the hemp down Monday. Damnable pen. Good bye.

Your aff. husband
John M Clay

Hope you enjoy the circus today.
[written in pencil]

6 p.m. race over half hour

Sally 2nd in the race, *Kitty* won & I would have preferred any other man in the nation to race to beat me but could not help it—5 heats—*Sally* behaved splendidly.[55]

The following year, John Clay had great success with a horse he called SB.

Maxwell House [Nashville]
7 p.m. 11th Oct. 1870

My Dear Wife,

I telegraphed you at 300 this afternoon through Breman & Swift that *Sauce Box* won the G. A. Stake—14 started, track muddy from a heavy rain last night, she slipped pretty bad, being a long strider & Ben who rode her had to get a good ways behind, swing to pulling her around the other & trying to keep her from falling down. At the head of the stretch *Mollie Cad* well ridden, but carrying 5 lbs overweight was at least 2 [yards] ahead of SB, but the ground getting a little less clipping SB made out to catch & beat her [by] 2 feet—Dudley was almost beside himself with joy & I feel encouraged . . . .

Love to all at home—Tell Lucretia SB has won a silk dress for her—Net value of G. A. Stake $1,175.

Your aff. husband
John M Clay[56]

John's long trips during the spring and summer were not always successful, and he was depressed much of the time. Josephine expressed concerns about his lifestyle while traveling, and his letters in response provide an insight into their relationship:

Eatontown, Monmouth County, New Jersey 19th June 1872

My Dear Wife,

Your unkind letter of the 15th was received and surprises me. I think you hardly do me

> justice when you quote the lines . . . if you will take the trouble to refer to my letter you will find "so we are where we ought to be." And which fairly interpreted means that I am sleeping & eating in a stable 900 miles from my own dear wife, living so rough that I am sorely tried to persevere in it and certainly, not altogether for myself for what I have, are you not a partner in it? And how would you like five studs, running in and out of their lots at home, fighting and killing one another? . . . if you will have patience and give me fair play I will continue to do the best I can . . . .
>
> I mean business you are the only wife I have or ever expect to have. I love you as I do myself, and would shed my blood for you if necessary, and am sure to be satisfied with whatever you do or have done in my absence, because I have confidence in you.
>
> My sincere love to the children, Your affectionate husband, John M. Clay.[57]

Josephine's response must have pleased John, because he wrote back to her:

> Your very welcome letter of the 21st reached me this forenoon. While you are making money at home, I am just expending money wholesale here. My expenses to this day from the time I left you are $1,500 and I have not thrown away one dollar. I am strongly tempted to sell every d____ one of the horses at auction this week and come home. But I am sure to do wrong anyway whether I go or stay.
>
> I have had and am likely to keep having your old pet—pure Neuralgia in both jaw bones, all the teeth, all the face & head bones & the right eye. I have had to get lodging away from the stable ¾ of a mile in a hamlet called Oceanport and I have some rest at night whereas previous to moving I had none till towards midnight.
>
> I am perfectly satisfied you will do all you can at home my dear wife for our interests, but I am almost sure the best I can do will avail nothing here.
>
> Thank heaven I have got Heaven to fall back on in all my troubles and they are plenty . . . .
>
> I am certain that whatever happens I train no more horses after this year & I wish next year had come—With love to all at home, including Lula when safely arrived I am as always.
>
> Your affectionate husband, John M. Clay[58]

John often complained about headaches and pain in the bones of his face which he called neuralgia. His drinking in the evening helped him sleep with the pain. On June 30, 1872 he wrote to Josephine, "I have a great piece of news. Thank merciful heaven my neuralgia was relieved by a good dentist. I had three teeth removed after the races and although Git [*La Gitana*] and Bally were both beaten, I felt better than if they had won."[59] He retired from active racing after this trip and devoted his time to breeding and raising stock.

A photograph of John and Josephine Clay shows the couple dressed in their best finery and gives the impression that Josephine was very much in charge, which indeed may have been the case.

Josephine played a major role in redirecting the business from racing to breeding Thoroughbreds with an annual sale of yearlings. On June 26, 1873, the "First Annual Sale of Yearlings, The Property of John M. Clay" took place in front of the Phoenix Hotel in Lexington.[60]

Fig. 6.6 Mr. and Mrs. John M. Clay

Ashland benefited from the success of a colt sold two years previously. *Survivor*, sold to John Chamberlain, ran in the inaugural Preakness in 1873 and won by ten lengths, a margin of victory that stood as the record until 2004.[61] In 1878, *Day Star* bred at Ashland and purchased by T. J. Nichols led the Kentucky Derby all the way to win by two lengths and clip one-half a second from the record set by *Aristides* in the inaugural running three years earlier. In six years of racing, *Day Star* won eleven of forty starts and earned $11,380.[62]

By 1878, Ashland's stock was aging. The stock book lists the following broodmares:

- Balloon foaled 19th February 1852, 26 years
- Skededdle foaled 6th February 1860, 18 years
- Georgie Woods foaled 1st March 1861, 17 years
- Squeez'em foaled 21st April 1869, 9 years
- La Gitana foaled 15th May 1869, 9 years
- Buff & Blue foaled 15th May 1873, 5 years
- Sly Boots foaled 3rd May 1870, 8 years

6.7 Monument to John M. Clay at Lexington Cemetery

To rebuild the farm, yearling fillies were not sold but retained as breeding stock, and the number of broodmares increased by one or two horses each year. During the following ten years, earnings for the farm were limited to a few yearlings offered for sale each year.[63]

In the early 1880s, John Clay's doctor told him that he had heart disease. Clay did not believe it and borrowed a book from another doctor and used it to try to prove to his doctor that he was in perfect health. But there followed a period during which John Clay began to have chest pain limiting his work on the farm.[64]

In June 1887, Josephine visited Independence, Missouri, where she had property in the city providing rental income. John Clay remained at Ashland, and they corresponded daily.

Ashland 2nd June 1887

Mrs. Clay

My Dear Wife,

According to promise I write to you today although I wrote yesterday morning about 10 o'c. Lula has tidied and made the house look bright and comfortable. She makes nice rolls every day which are excellent, and she & little Jose [Josephine Clay Simpson] could not be more kind and attentive to my wants & comfort . . . .

Our equine family are tolerably fair now. The Slashes eats 8 qts of oats daily & is in good spirits. I cease the quinine from today. I have no answer yet from Harper about Ginger Pop.

But have written him again. I hope and trust you and Nettie have arrived at Independence. Don't let the real estate agents bully you.

Most affectionately
John M Clay[65]

On August 10, 1887, John Clay visited Lexington to pay his taxes and told his friends he was elated over the prospects for his yearlings. He returned about 3 o'clock and supervised a plumber fixing a water pump in a field. Without warning he fell, and the workman said there were no signs of life. He died suddenly from a stroke at age sixty-six. The local newspaper published an article the following day with the title "The Last Child of 'Harry of the West' Joins the Silent Majority."

> Another of Fayette county's most prominent citizens passed away suddenly this afternoon .... He commenced horse-racing in 1847 and has bred more high-class horses than any other man in the State with his limited number of stock. Among others, he bred *Pocahontas, Balloon, True Blue, Sailor Boy, Ballot, Ginger, Daniel Boone, Kentucky, Victory, Sly Boots, La Sylphide, Sly Dance, Sylph, Charley Ball, Arcola, Lodi, Blue Bonnet, Waterloo, Linktum, Austerlitz, Star Davis, Ban Cloche* and many others .... His wealth is unknown; for although he has made large amounts by the sale of stock, he had the peculiar character of the Clays, which made them all poor financiers.[66]

Josephine inherited his house, acreage, and twelve broodmares, all descendants of Henry Clay's broodmares *Magnolia* and *Margaret Wood*. John M. Clay was buried at the Lexington Cemetery with a large monument at the bottom of the hill where his mother and father were buried.

Chapter 7

Owner, Manager and Writer

For your reign will, like the winter of life,
Yield to a spring radiantly fair.[1]

After the death of her husband, Josephine Clay assumed the ownership and management of Ashland Stock Farm. She tried to lower expectations for her management of the farm by describing herself as an "incompetent doing her best to continue the traditions of great men." She said: "I know that in the continuance of the business, a hard task lay before me, and success is almost impossible." She used this humble approach to her new responsibilities to gain the support of horse owners and buyers as the first woman to manage a Thoroughbred horse farm in Kentucky.[2] Josephine Clay focused her life almost exclusively on managing the horse farm, leaving social activities to others, quite unusual for a prominent woman in Lexington at that time.

Women were not eligible to join the Jockey Club of New York, the Lexington Racing Association, and the other clubs and organizations that dominated the industry. To stay in touch with the inner circle of horse farm managers in the bluegrass, Josephine began stopping at the Phoenix Hotel in downtown Lexington, where horsemen often congregated. On more than a few occasions, she joined the poker games.[3]

Slowly, she was accepted by the horsemen for her knowledge of pedigrees and racing history; but it was probably her communications skills and distinctive way of treating her horses like pets which distinguished her from other breeders. One article published in New York and reprinted in the Lexington newpaper said she was often seen riding in her fields wearing a broad-brimmed straw hat. She would stop at each horse, dismount, pet the horse, and appear to talk softly saying affectionate things, while the horse would take a bite from her hat. She told the reporter from the New York *Morning Telegraph* that she only paid a quarter for her hats.[4] After reading the article, some of the local farmers commented that she preferred speaking to horses rather than people.[5]

She did not train or race horses; rather she sold the colts to others for racing, while keeping the fillies to enhance the breeding operation. She managed to increase the number of broodmares at Ashland Stock Farm from the dozen she inherited to over fifty.

In 1889, she sold a yearling colt named *Riley* at a public sale for $950. When *Riley* won the Kentucky Derby in 1890, ridden by Isaac Murphy, the famous African-American jockey, she received national news coverage. New York reporters asked to visit her farm, and she became the subject of articles in the *Morning Telegraph*, *The Thoroughbred Record*, and *Turf, Field and Farm*. Headlines that appeared in the sports pages of New York newspapers include "Stock

Farm Successfully Conducted By a Woman" and "Mrs. Clay, the World's Most Successful Horse Breeder."[6]

As Josephine Clay's reputation increased throughout the country, her farm income began to show the results of her efforts. In 1895, at Morris Park in New York, one of her yearlings brought $8,200, a record amount at the time, and her horses sold for an average of $3,500. She reinvested the proceeds of her horse sales in land and improvements. Each year she added fencing, buildings, and other improvements to her property and purchased several farms farther out the Tates Creek Pike.[7] The size and scope of the properties she purchased with her earnings enhanced her reputation as a wealthy member of the Lexington community.

Her attention to detail, hard work, and rapport with her horses was described in a speech, "Women in the Professions," Josephine Clay prepared for the International Conference of Women, in Toronto, Canada, in 1903. She was unable to attend the conference, and her speech was read for her and reprinted in a number of newspapers, including the *Kansas City Star* and *Lexington Herald*:

> I know well that in the continuance of the business in which my husband long had been engaged, a hard task lay before me and to be successful seemed almost beyond the pale of possibility—men of experience had wrecked fortunes and failed conspicuously. But feeling pledged to the difficult undertaking, I resolved to do my best and to rely absolutely on myself—to paddle my own canoe; and if the craft went down, to sink with her. I believed then, as I do now, that when we really are trying to do what is right, an inspiration comes from above to help and console, or I would have made more mistakes than I did.
>
> Certainly, so far as I knew how, the stock was well cared for. To the many things my attention was given personally, I was not often disconcerted. I made a study of turf registers and became well acquainted with horse ancestry. A turf correspondent, after a visit to my place published that he had for twenty years been writing about horses, but the way Mrs. Clay rattled off direct pedigrees, throwing in collaterals, made his head swim.
>
> Except for sailors, there are no people on earth so deeply tied to superstition as those whose business is to work with race horses. For example, when with breathless haste the communication of a new baby is made, with haste equally breathless, I would hurry to welcome the little stranger and to pass judgment on his "points"—discernible to the practiced eye, even at a tender age. But the moment I was inside the door—closed secure to ensure quiet for mamma and infant, anxious voices would whisper "Stop, Stop." This interruption was to give the young foal the opportunity to wriggle up and rub his head against me, the owner. If this was done of his own accord, it was the sign and seal that he was predestined to great renown on the turf. Otherwise, he was counterfeit and not worth bringing up.
>
> At one time having trouble with my eyes, I was away several weeks for treatment, returning home with glasses. The stock I first visited were about a dozen brood mares at large in a pasture. Glad to see them and expecting a show of reciprocal feeling, I was shocked to observe that their unanimous movement toward me was suddenly and decisively checked, disdainful glances toward me shooting from their bright eyes. I understand the talk of horses and they understand my language. "Ladies, dear ladies," I implored, deeply hurt, "are you not glad to see me?" "The matter is," answered Lorna Alta, vindictively, "you went away from us, and you have come back to us in barnacles. We don't like it." "I don't like it

> either," I replied, "but it is something I can't help." "Take them off," demanded Clotaire, "if you want us to have respect for you." In my pocket out of sight went the offending glasses, and in a moment they were all frisking around me, testifying the fondest affection. Of all the creatures, the Thoroughbred horse is the most conservative, the most adverse to innovations and obstinately predetermined to let well enough alone.
>
> The stock book was kept by myself, and without assistance, I edited my annual catalogue and made my yearly report to the Jockey Club of New York City. I registered the foals and superintended the preparation of the yearlings for the Spring sales—a busy life but I had my innings. One yearling colt sold for $8,200. And better still, my horses gave a good account of themselves when put to racing. Three of my colts won derby honors and I had a colt win the rich Realization Stakes of $11,000.[8] Curate won a cup race—the longest distance race now run—at New Orleans in record breaking time. Besides, many good stakes winners—Semper Ego, Woden, Jove, Precinct and Coligny were renowned steeplechasers. El Cuchillo was last year considered the best steeplechaser in the world and was sent to France, but died soon after completing the voyage.
>
> To keep nothing back—I make the admission steeped in humiliation—I have never been able to master the multiplication table though I always well remember a salutary lesson learned from one of my school books:
>
> And oh, if fortune fill thy sail
> With more than a propitious gale,
> Take half thy canvas in.[9]

During Josephine's most active years in the horse business, she wrote romantic novels. Lippincott & Co. in Philadelphia published her first book in 1873 composed of two stories with the title *What Will the World Say?: A Novel of Every-Day Life; and Only a Woman.* Josephine used an appropriate pen name, Ojos Morenos (dark eyes). The book was dedicated to Capt. Douglas Ottinger of the U. S. Coast Guard Revenue Cutter *Frolic*, a friend and hero to Josephine and her father.[10]

Both of the stories take place in England. *What Will the World Say?* is the story of a young lady, Miss Suzette, from a struggling family. Her father is killed in a train accident, but she overcomes her low social status as an orphan when she is adopted by a famous noblewoman, Lady Margaret. In a standard Victorian romance, she later falls in love and marries the Earl of Huntington.

Only a Woman is a more unusual story with a feminist theme. The story is told by a rector about "how loving, true and strong a woman can be." When a family tries to arrange a marriage for their beautiful daughter to an older nobleman, she runs away with a circus company and falls in love with a tiger trainer. When her lover is attacked and killed by his animals, she substitutes for him in the circus, showing how a woman can successfully perform the most dangerous job in the circus. In the end, she returns home to find all the members of her family have died, and she is the Countess of Lansdow and a tiger trainer.

Her second book, *Some Little Angels Still Left: A Novel,* is dedicated "to the beloved memory of John M. Clay . . . inscribed with the eternal truth of my heart's best affections." It was published in 1893 by Robert Clark & Co. of Cincinnati. The story is a racing romance blended with Crimean War scenes. According to a review of the second edition in *The Thoroughbred Record*, it was the first novel ever written that features a horse, *Don Juan*, as a main character. It describes the City of Paris Handicap Race involving English and French owners where *Don Juan* and his jockey are killed. After

Fig. 7.1 Josephine Clay Pictured with "Friends" in *Frank Logan*. *The Abbey Press*

the tragic result of the race, the heroine is transformed into a strong, successful woman. *The Thoroughbred Record* commented: "Turf men and breeders of the Thoroughbred . . . feel an unusual interest in this book on account of Mrs. Clay's well-known fondness for the Thoroughbred—Ashland, of which she is the proprietress, being one of the great Kentucky nurseries . . . . The story is a charmingly written romance with an artistic construction and literary merit which make it a welcome addition to any library."[11]

In 1899, the romance *Uncle Phil* was published by F. Tennyson Neely of New York and London, and proved to be her most popular novel. It was dedicated to her ancestor, Brig. Gen. William Russell, who served in George Washington's Grand Army of the Republic. Josephine's experiences in Monterey and Vicksburg are reflected in the book. The story centers on a Virginia gentleman, with a young, beautiful daughter, who loses his estate after he backs the wrong candidate in an election. They are forced to move to California, where he accepts a position as director of customs in a small Spanish town. The heroine falls in love with an older friend of her father who later becomes a Confederate officer. She also befriends a young army lieutenant and family friend living in a near-by fort. Both leave to fight in the Civil War. When her father dies, her stepmother encourages her to marry a family friend, who treats her badly. She follows her husband to Vicksburg where she meets both of her former lovers but cannot be unfaithful to her marriage. After her husband and the two other men in her life are killed in the fighting, she moves to Nashville with the family servant, Uncle Phil, where she begins a successful career as a legal assistant. A revised edition of the novel was published in 1901 by The Abbey Press, New York, the successor to the original publisher.[12]

In 1901, the novel *Frank Logan*, dedicated to Henry Clay, was also published by The Abbey Press. The cover is blue and gold, showing Kentucky's coat of arms. The front piece shows the author in a scene of four on her stock farm; three are equine Thoroughbreds. The six foot one inch Kentucky

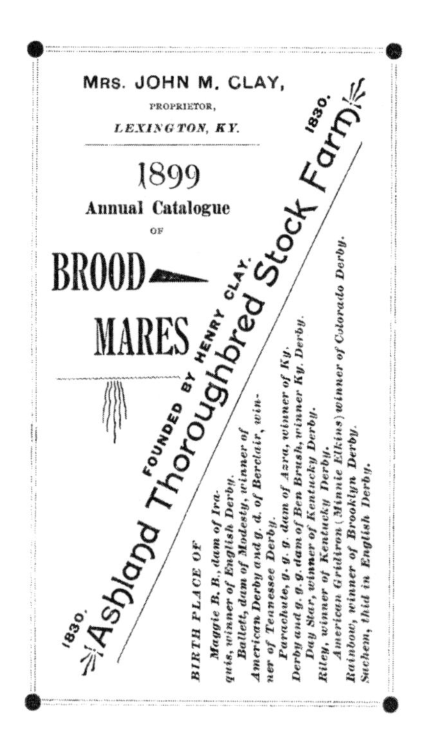

MRS. JOHN M. CLAY,
PROPRIETOR,
LEXINGTON, KY.

1899
Annual Catalogue
OF
BROOD MARES

1830. Ashland Thoroughbred Stock Farm 1830.
FOUNDED BY HENRY CLAY.

BIRTH PLACE OF
Maggie B. B., dam of Iraquis, winner of English Derby.
Ballett, dam of Modesty, winner of American Derby and g. d. of Berclair, winner of Tennessee Derby.
Parachute, g. g. g. dam of Azra, winner of Ky. Derby and g. g. g. dam of Ben Brush, winner Ky. Derby.
Day Star, winner of Kentucky Derby.
Riley, winner of Kentucky Derby.
American Gridiron (Minnie Elkins) winner of Colorado Derby.
Rainbow, winner of Brooklyn Derby.
Sachem, thid in English Derby.

The following Yearlings from the Ashland Thoroughbred Farm will be sold at auction by the American Horse Exchange, New York,

FRIDAY, JUNE 30, 1899, AT 1 O'CLOCK.

Bay colt Lares (brother to Loki) by Logic, dam The Slashes.
Bay colt Trenct the Mere (half brother to Rainbow and Bright Phoebus) by Carlsbad, dam Buff and Blue.
Bay colt Chaplain (dam sister to Riley) by Carlsbad, dam Genoa.
Bay colt Luego (brother to Linstock) by Logic, dam Blue Stocking.
Brown colt Cinqueport (dam half sister to La Sylphide and Koloolah) by Carlsbad, dam Logie.
Brown colt Callear (g. g. son of Buff and Blue, by Carlsbad, dam Loire.
Brown colt Bon Coeur (grandson to La Sylphide), by Carlsbad, dam Semper d'Or.
Bay filly Loving Kindness (sister to Latch Key) by Logic, dam Lady Relief.
Bay filly Lochaber (g. g. daughter to Buff and Blue) by Carlsbad, dam Bonnets o' Blue.
Bay filly Corral (granddaughter to Bonnets o' Blue), by Carlsbad, dam Jacket o' Blue.
Chestnut filly Coralie (g. g. daughter to Sylph) by Carlsbad, dam Lora.

Fig. 7.2 The 1899 "Annual Catalogue of Brood Mares" for Ashland Stock Farm

hero of the novel is modeled after Henry Clay and tells the story of how Henry Clay might have conducted himself in the Civil War.

The story deals graphically with feuding Kentucky families during the period of the Civil War in which the hero, Frank Logan, a general in the Union army, and Margaret Toliver, an equally strong heroine from a rival family, meet and fall in love. General Logan hunts down Capt. Sue Munday, the celebrated outlaw leader of a rebel band in Kentucky during the Civil War. Josephine must have been aware of the real life Captain Munday who led a raid on Woodburn Farm and rode off with the famous stallion *Asteroid.*[13] She added a fictional twist to a story which was well known in Kentucky at that time. In her story, the Federal troops are afraid of the magical powers of a girl leading the rebels who could not be killed by bullets. General Logan captures and undresses the Captain Munday finding a young boy leading the rebel outlaws.[14]

Josephine's novels are difficult to read today because of the flowery language and romantic plots, in the style of the Victorian period. Her scenes have outstanding detail, even if the story occurs in a foreign country she had not visited. She is always convincing when writing about Thoroughbreds, and her use of descriptive language demonstrates the education she received from reading great books. *Uncle Phil* is important for what it reveals about her life and her impressions of the Civil War.

Josephine also used her writing and communications skills to increase the reputation of her farm. Her annual catalogues were different from other farms and highly regarded for creative design, the level of background information about the horses being sold, and stories from the history of racing.[15]

In 1899, the record of the top ten horses bred by Josephine Clay, after Ashland Stock Farm came into her possession, was published in New York by the *Morning Telegraph*.

Table 1. The Ten Most Successful Horses Bred by Josephine Clay. ***Morning Telegraph*, ca. 1899**

Name	Times Started	Times First	Times Second	Times Third	Amount Won
Riley	65	30	17	5	$42,715
Bright Phoebus	24	9	4	3	$40,440
Kaloolah	101	24	10	19	$33,623
Semper Ego	59	17	10	11	$16,335
Rainbow	38	3	6	6	$10,130
Semper Rex	24	7	1	4	$10,110
Monita Hardy	73	16	13	12	$7,610
Semper Hidele	17	6	1	2	$6,641
Kinesem	37	11	8	3	$5,345
Ban Cloche	47	4	9	6	$5,169
Totals	**485**	**127**	**79**	**71**	**$178,118**

The ten most successful horses she bred won 25 percent of their 485 races, with total winnings of $178,118.[16]

As the century ended, Josephine placed an article in her scrapbook describing how millionaires were replacing Kentuckians in the ownership of major horse farms of the bluegrass. It listed the amounts paid for Kentucky farms including August Belmont, $500,000; Foxhall & Keene, $500,000; J. B. Hagin $500,000; and W.C. Whitney, $300,000.[17]

Each year the top bluegrass farms, including Ashland, sent shipments of yearlings to sell in New York. Due to the increased interest in racing, prices received for Thoroughbreds showed dramatic increases, but the turn of the century proved to be a high point in the boom-and-bust cycle of the Thoroughbred horse business in America.

Prices received for Thoroughbred horses declined, and Josephine, whose eyesight was failing from cataracts, began to think about retiring from the horse business. In 1903, fifteen years after becoming the owner of Ashland Stock Farm, she decided to sell her stock. On November 18, 1903, she offered to sell 38 of the 52 horses she owned and to lease most of her land.[18]

The catalog for the sale contained the following statement:

> Henry Clay of Ashland was first called the Great Commoner for his active championage (sic) of the People's cause, in resisting with all his might the passing of the Alien and Sedition Act, and by that name he still lives in the hearts of his countrymen.

Fig. 7.3 Josephine Clay and grooms with *La Sylphide, Buff and Blue,* and *Bonnet o'Blue* at Ashland on Tates Creek Pike. *Turf, Field & Farm, 1899.*

Magnolia and Margaret Wood were presented to him in 1845 by Messrs. Mercer and Hampton. Yorkshire was presented to him in 1846 by Commodore Morgan. The descendants of this stock, by their excellence, soon made the Ashland famous, under the management of his son, John M. Clay. This gentleman was long on the turf and one of its ornaments, noted for unfailing integrity and love for fairness—any deviation from the strict code of justice would call down his unqualified disapproval.

His horses were never asked to race when not in condition: many persons will yet remember the animated, even joyous, appearance of his horses when brought on the course for their races, their coats shining with the living gloss of health.

And it was a joy to see him at home among his horses. He inherited his father's magic voice, and the animals would lift up their heads to catch the music of its tones. But the time came when I went out among the horses alone. They all crowded near with sorrowful eyes, instinct telling them of the irreparable loss. With my arms around old Skedaddle's neck, I promised: "We will all stay together." And faithfully I have tried my very best to care for them. No weather has been too inclement to prevent me from personally seeing that their needs were supplied. But sixteen years have outlasted health and strength, and I now can no longer care for them properly, and painful to me as it is, for their own well-being, I must turn them over to stronger and more competent hands.

For this reason I have yielded to the hard necessity of a dispersal sale. But I hope, with all

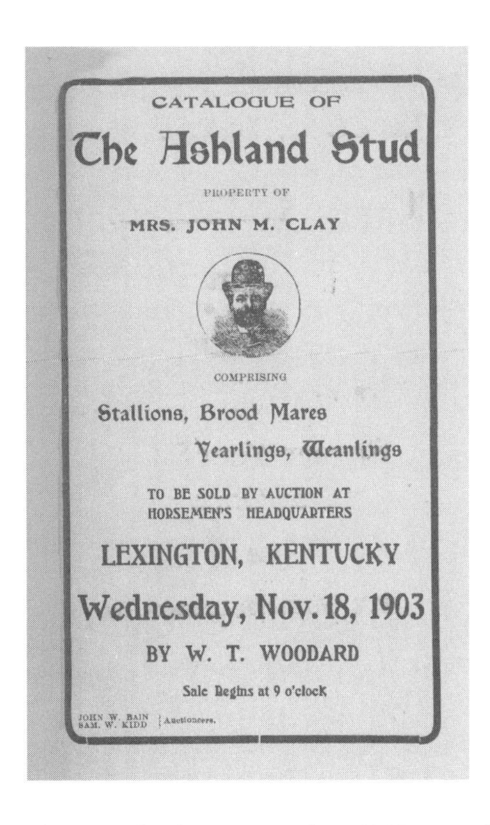

Fig.7.4 W. T. Woodard Catalogue of Sales, November, 1903. *Keeneland Association Library*

my heart, that every one of the stock may fall into appreciative hands, and yet for me is reserved the pleasure of hearing of its continued and brilliant success.

Josephine Clay[19]

The sale occurred on a cold, raw day, and despite important buyers that included Lucien Appleby from New York, O. H. Chenault of Spendthrift Farm, and Col. E. F. Clay of Runnymede Farm, the sale was a failure. There were two other important horse sales that day in Lexington and the market collapsed. According to the *New York Times*, thirty-eight horses sold for a total of $7,790, an average of $205 a head. Four hundred acres were leased for five years to W. W. D. Stokes from New York, the owner of Patchen Wilkes Farm, to be used for grazing horses. The residence and twenty-five acres were reserved by Josephine Clay for her use.[20] In the publicity following the sale, she tried to follow a favorite saying that ended her horse catalogues: "to show well, to brag little, to crow gently if in luck; and to pay up, own up and shut up when beaten, are the virtues of a sporting man [and woman]."

Chapter 8

Family Legacy

In the wild wind's moan as it winds o'er the lea,
In the rustling of leaves as they fall from the tree.[1]

When Josephine Clay's father, Col. William H. Russell, separated from his family in 1860, he moved to Kansas, which had been admitted as a new state of the Union permitting slavery. The decision on slavery split the Whig Party, with most Northern Whigs going over to the Republicans, who opposed the expansion of slavery. Russell supported the Republicans and campaigned in 1860 for the election of Abraham Lincoln to the presidency. Lincoln's success finally brought Russell a long-sought-after government appointment. President Lincoln appointed Russell to be U. S. Consul at Trinidad de Cuba, where he served throughout the Civil War.[2]

After Lincoln's assassination, he was replaced and returned to live in Washington, D. C., where he lobbied to be appointed Minister to Cuba. His application to President Andrew Johnson was supported by a letter of recommendation from a political colleague Robert J. Walker, the United States financial agent to Europe during the Civil War and a former governor of Kansas:

> [Russell] was appointed by Mr. Lincoln, U. S. Consul at Trinidad de Cuba, which office he held until after the assassination, receiving the plaudits of all for the faithful manner in which he discharged his duties, especially for his successful effort to rescue the [steamship] Joseph Maxwell from the claims of the Spanish government, she being a prize of the Confederate steamer Sumpter. His record is spotless, and I most earnestly commend him to your favorable consideration.
>
> Yours very respectfully, R. J. WALKER.

Colonel Russell was considered an "old school" Whig who had passed from favor, and he was unable to obtain another appointment. He stayed in Washington until he died on October 13, 1873, and was buried in Oak Lawn Cemetery, Georgetown, D. C.[3]

The History of Callaway County begins a description of Colonel Russell's life as follows: "One of the most remarkable men of early times was the person whose name is at the head of this memoir [William H. Russell], and who spent most of his professional life in Fulton, Callaway County, Missouri. His entire life was one of excitement, daring and adventure, and in the hands of a ready, imaginative writer, would furnish ample material for a good sized volume of romance."[4]

Fig. 8.1 Minor Simpson

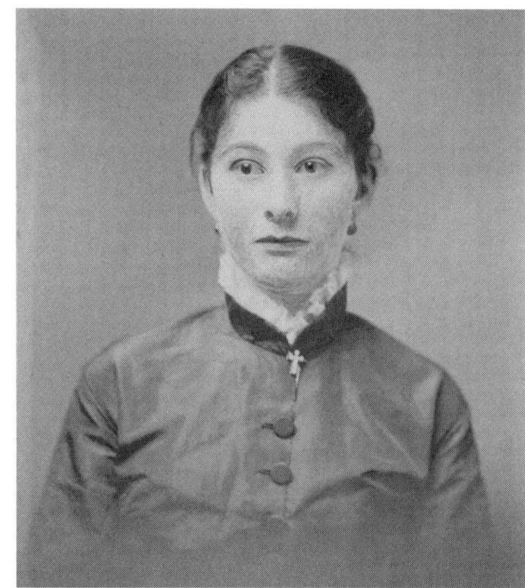

Fig 8.2 Lucretia Erwin

Josephine's travels with her father at an early age were an important influence on her. She learned to admire his sense of exploration and adventure, and when she was older, she was attracted to men like her father. As a teenager, she was infatuated with Douglas Ottinger, an older Coast Guard captain and adventurer. She married Eugene Erwin, who became the dynamic leader of a regiment in the Civil War. Her second marriage to John M. Clay brought her to the high-risk-profession of Thoroughbred breeding and racing. After his death, she pursued her own career to "paddle my own canoe . . . .," and she was more successful than her father.

Zaenett Russell moved with her daughter and grandchildren to Lexington in 1866 and lived with them at Ashland on Tates Creek Pike. There is no information about her life in Lexington except that she died in 1880. Her funeral took place at the Main Street Christian Church, and she was buried at the Lexington Cemetery in the Russell family lot near her brother-in-law Thomas A. Russell.[5]

Josephine Clay urged her daughters to be careful about their choice of a husband, and was critical when they became interested in much older men.[6] Lula was the first to marry and chose a local farmer, Minor Young Simpson.

Simpson, who had worked breaking hemp at Ashland when he was a teenager, inherited his father's farm and provided hay and other supplies to Ashland for the horses.[7] His farm was several miles farther out the Tates Creek Pike on East Hickman Creek. At age forty, Minor was almost twice Lula's age and close to her mother's age. He was a thin man with a long beard that makes his face look square with a serious, intent look. In 1875, he became romantically interested in Lula, but Josephine was not enthusiastic about having him as a son-in-law. A photograph of Lula reveals that she was an attractive young woman with a distracted gaze. Apparently, Lula was quite shy and considered herself to be plain. She was flattered by Minor Simpson's interest.

Fig. 8.3 Josephine Clay in Her Study at Ashland on Tates Creek Road

When Simpson asked Lula to marry him, Maj. Henry Clay McDowell, who was married to Anne Clay, the daughter of Henry Clay, Jr., supported the engagement. He pointed out that Simpson had worked hard to obtain a degree from Georgetown College, and after his father died at an early age, successfully managed his family's farm.[8] Over time, John and Josephine Clay accepted Lula's engagement. On February 6, 1876, Lucretia Erwin married Minor Simpson and moved to the Simpson family's farm. Their first child, John Morrison Simpson, was born in 1877. At age eighteen, he tragically died after contracting pneumonia following a Kentucky University track meet. Minor and Lucretia Simpson had three more children: Josephine Clay Simpson was born in 1878; Eugene Erwin Simpson in 1880; and my father, Henry Clay Simpson, in 1896.

In 1887, Josephine's second daughter, Nettie, married Howard H. Gratz, editor and publisher of one of Lexington's first newspapers, which had been founded by his family. At age sixty-three, he was more than twice Nettie's age of thirty. Nettie lived only two years after their marriage. She died suddenly of cerebral meningitis at their home on North Limestone in Lexington.

In 1890, Josephine's third daughter Mary married Matthew William Anderson, a well respected banker living in Independence, Missouri. At age fifty-four, he was within a year of Josephine's age and twenty-five years older than Mary. They married and lived in Independence and had three sons, Henry Clay Anderson in 1891, George Anderson in 1893 (who died as an infant), and Matthew William Anderson, Jr. in 1895.

In 1898, Josephine Clay purchased a one-half interest in Minor Simpson's 370-acre farm on the Tates Creek Pike. The partnership with her son-in-law must have been successful, because in 1903 she invited the Minor Simpson family to move to her home now called Ashland on Tates Creek Road.

With the expansion of Lexington, the Tates Creek toll pike owned by John M. Clay and other farmers became a public road. To encourage the building of public roads, Josephine deeded a stone quarry to the county government with the provision that the ownership revert back to her if it was not used for that purpose.[9]

8.5 Josephine Clay with Family at Ashland on Tates Creek Road, 1900
Rear Left to Right: Mary Webster Anderson, Eugene Erwin Simpson, Josephine Clay Simpson, Lucretia Erwin Simpson, and Josephine Clay.
Middle: Matthew William Anderson, Minor Simpson
Front: Henry Clay Anderson, Matthew William Anderson, Jr. and Henry Clay Simpson

Josephine continued to manage a few broodmares with Simpson family help on a small portion of her property and rented the balance of her horse farm. The Simpson family lived on the second floor in three bedrooms.

Josephine had a new wing built for her use that included a separate bedroom and bath on the first floor, and a study on the second floor. She used the study for writing, where she was surrounded by Clay and Russell family antiques and papers.

Ashland on Tates Creek Road was often filled with children and visiting grandchildren. Josephine enjoyed her grandchildren and wrote in her story "Honors are Easy:" "Thanks to the good God! . . . the possession of a spontaneous blessing, not purchasable by the aggregate gold of the universe, in the all-absorbing, self-sacrificing devotion of a youthful granddaughter. . . ."[10] In a photograph of her family taken in 1900, the two "older" sons-in-law of Josephine Clay were seated while she was standing on the right.

After Josephine Clay decided to sell her horses, she addressed a long-postponed medical problem by agreeing to have a doctor in Louisville treat the cataracts that damaged her vision. She traveled to Louisville early in 1905, and his treatment was a success. During the trip she visited an older friend and former neighbor she called "my dear little sweetheart, cousin Jimmie." The seventy-nine-year-old widow, Mrs. James Ann Pearce Pindell, who was named for her father James, was being cared for at the St. Joseph's Infirmary in Louisville. She was considered a Clay family cousin after she married Henry Clay Pindell, a grandson of Eliza Hart, the older sister of Mrs. Henry Clay.[11] After Josephine returned to Ashland, she wrote a letter describing her plans for the coming year.

Ashland Thoroughbred Stock Farm
near Lexington, Kentucky
Mrs. John M. Clay, Proprietor

30 March, 1905

My Dear Little Sweetheart:

I am home just four weeks today, and you would be surprised at the change in me; I am heavier than ever before, got a good color, and in radiant spirits now that I am not an extinct luminary. I have been so busy and accomplished so much. I have made a most excellent arrangement about my broodmares—most of them were taken from Ashland today to be returned 1st July; the prospective foals are sold, to be taken 1st October 1906. The tobacco crop is sold—I got $3000 for my half-interest. The hemp crop is not yet ready for sale. I had but one yearling and I have sold and delivered him. I have bought a house and lot in Lex. on Upper Street for just a scrap of paper directing the Fayette National Bank to pay to the trustees of the First Presbyterian Church $4,000. [12] The lot is central and will soon be valuable—the house is old and not much account, but I am going to have it repaired for a tenant. I have had my new Hazelton piano tuned and have learned two new pieces, and I work a little every day on the Historical Romance.[13]

About 1st May, I am as you know, to go back to Dr. Ray; when he gets through with me I fear I will have to go out to Independence, Missouri, where I have some property—for two years I have been resisting the extension of brick streets and asphalt side-walks, and a special tax of twenty-two hundred dollars. Taxes are so dreadfully irritating—my taxes here have been raised from $800 to $1000—just think of it—there is no way to help myself, and being a woman I can't even swear.

Since getting home I have been made as much of as if I had been "sweet Alice,"[14] and to express my thanks am going to have a lawn fete, I expect directly after Easter, but I think now to postpone it till I get back from Louisville (praying I will not be forced to go to Mo.). Most people think a band (inferior), sandwiches and lemonade are sufficient for a lawn fete; but I am going to give my people plenty to eat of the best, and Saxton's band, and some very fine singing.

I went to Shaffer's music store to see if I could get the music of some old songs my father use to sing, I only knew the names. He had the songs and said he did not think they could be found anywhere else in America, as they have been out of print fifty years. To have the singing well done it will be under professional direction. My dear little sweetheart I would like so much for you to hear this singing. When I go to Louisville perhaps I can persuade you to make me a visit. I promise to wait on you myself and anybody I take in charge will be certain to have a lively time—that's my specialty. Give my love to Cousin Sue, I will try to write to her soon. I have been so fidgety since the horses were taken away that, as a solace, I am writing to you. Lula joins me in much love and in the hope you are keeping well. You must not be ailing when I go down for what would I do—you are the only sweetheart I've got.

Affectionately, Josephine Clay[15]

Josephine's lawn party was held on Saturday afternoon June 3rd at 5. p.m. at Ashland on Tates Creek Road. A newspaper article about the party listed about 150 guests and described it as "the foremost party for the year in the Blue Grass."

> The lawn is a picture at all times with its groups of pines and wild cherry trees, lilac hedge, roses and flower beds, and had the addition of many colored lanterns, and flags flying in the breeze...on the perfect June day. The front veranda and canopy over the refreshment table on the lawn were hung in buff and blue, the Clay racing colors... At the entrance to the lawn a rug was spread and Mrs. Clay received her guests assisted by her daughter Mrs. Minor Simpson and Mr. Simpson and her grandchildren. Saxton & Trost's orchestra, stationed under a group of trees played a pleasant accompaniment . . .and a music program was given to each guest... a part of the evening was devoted to a little concert that featured six vocalists . . . . A feast was served buffet style.

The party concluded with all the guests singing "Old Kentucky Home," "I've Got a Feelin' For You," and "Good Bye, Sweetheart, Good Bye."[16]

Josephine continued her active correspondence with Mrs. Pindell and described an incident in church.

Ashland Thoroughbred Stock Farm
near Lexington, Kentucky
Mrs. John M. Clay, Proprietor

23 April, 1905

My Own Dear Cousin Jimmie,

I was delighted to receive your pretty Easter greeting, and am writing to tell you so. I got it from the P. O. on my homeward way from church, where, I experienced a very curious misadventure. Being Rector Lee's last sermon before his departure for Los Angeles, his new pastorate, the building was crowded.[17] After services as I was making my way with such haste as I could down the long isle I was brought to a stand-still by [my granddaughter] Josephine's[18] voice, it was agitated—saying: Stop, Bonny, your dust ruffle has come loose. So it had; being put together with chain-stich [sic] when trod on it gave way and unraveled, and had it been let alone I would soon have measured many yards from tip to tip.

But Josephine, fortunately just behind, and a resourceful child—knowing that the dust ruffle and I ought to be as one and could not be separated without regret—had gathered it up, looping it in festoons over her arm and it was in no one's way; but the trailing thread, unobserved, so silently had it pursued its meandering course entwining itself about the feet of various persons, obstructing navigation, causing discontent. These persons stood, shuffling uncomfortable with the harrowing fear that the humiliation was in store for them of being forced to stoop down to obtain their liberation. Break the thread, I promptly advised and joy soon reigned. But my own probation [was] not quite at an end, Josephine, feeling that she had done enough, when we got into the carriage, deposited the mass on my lap, and I was quickly over-flowing with billows of fluted lace-work. Do not imagine, Cousin Jimmie, that this occurrence occasioned me the least embarrassment. Among [my] own people I am in a class by myself and can do as I like. I could even steal a horse, and nothing [would be] said, while many excellent persons would excite unpleasant comments if they even looked at a bridle.

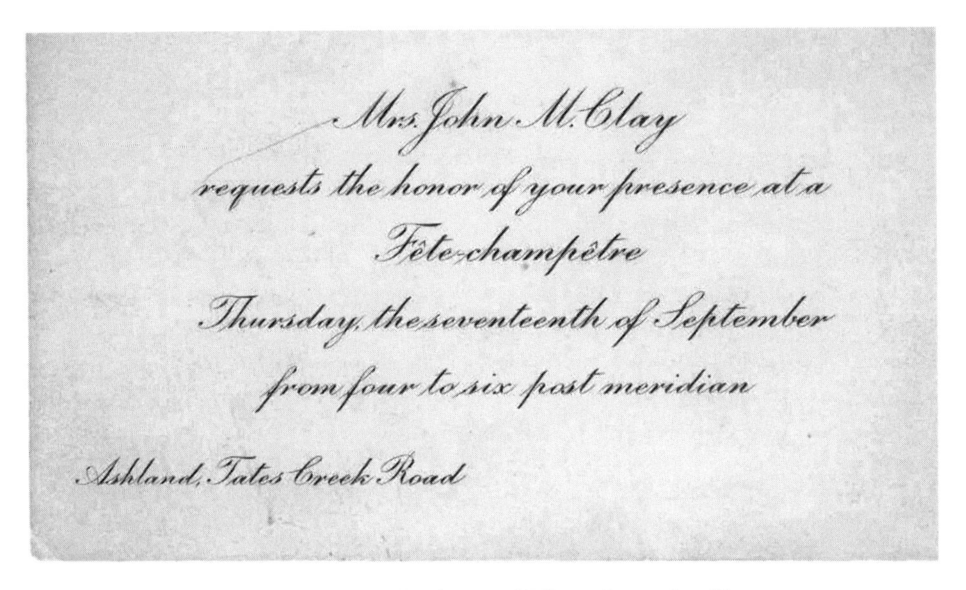
Mrs. John M. Clay
requests the honor of your presence at a
Fête-champêtre
Thursday, the seventeenth of September
from four to six post meridian

Ashland, Tates Creek Road

Figure 8.6 Invitation to "Fête-champêtre"

It will be hard to replace Mr. Lee; he has never preached to empty pews, and he has attracted the masculine element although he right often got after it with a sharp stick. The women, he said, were good enough—it was the men who needed the preachment. But in giving him up, there is one circumstance to lighten the woe of his congregation, namely, his children. For perhaps good and sufficient reasons, preacher's children have obtained an unenviable notoriety for badness, but Mr. Lee's progeny are, it is said, bad beyond comparison. While at the Phoenix, the following took place: Stop, boys, implored a voice, you'll kill yourselves! Don't stop them! Hurriedly put in another voice, if they do kill themselves it will be a relief to a long suffering community.

You may expect to see me tomorrow week, at which time I was directed by Dr. Ray to come back to Louisville.

My eyes are now doing me very good service, but I want them for all they are worth, and I am not going to set myself up against the doctor.

You must make it a point to be at your best when I come down, I am expecting so much pleasure in seeing you. I wish you were here to see the row of lilacs set out by Mr. Clay's mother, now in magnificent bloom, and a sight worth coming a long distance to see. Yesterday enough of the white and purple blossoms were sent to decorate the altar, baptismal font and the altar rail profusely [at] our church, and they cannot be missed.

Lula sends love, and my dear little sweetheart you will

Know I am always Lovingly Yours, Josephine Clay[19]

Many people in Lexington who heard about her party inquired about when she would have another party. Josephine decided to organize another lawn party in the fall to include a larger number of guests. She called it a "fête-champêtre." Over 200 prominent guests from the town attended according a newspaper article. The food included Maryland ham after Mrs. Henry Clay's recipe, and Ashland's silver racing trophies were on the serving table with buff and blue decorating the front veranda. A program of music was again played by Saxton & Trost's band.

Josephine Clay spent much of her time managing the properties she acquired and adding to her holdings. Her most significant transaction took place in 1909 when she purchased the Pettit farm for $15,970 on the Mount Tabor Road, adding 175 acres and another substantial home, Harmony Hall, to the farm she inherited from John M. Clay. Including the land she purchased farther out the Tates Creek Road, her ownership totaled over 1,200 acres. She purchased three properties from the Northern Bank in downtown Lexington, a brick dwelling and two lots. She managed these real estate investments as rental properties.[20]

A Russell cousin researching family history wrote to Josephine to obtain information about her great-grandmother, Abigail Millar. (Her daughter Deborah Montgomery Allen married Josephine's grand-father Robert Spotswood Russell.) In a letter responding to the request, Josephine replied: "I have been very busy here and can not help you. I have found that studying pedigrees of four feet more profitable than two."[21]

The exact date is not known but around 1910 Josephine Clay's life changed. She broke her hip, and her activities were restricted. She spent most of her time in the new bedroom and study which she had added to her home. She researched many possible subjects for newspaper articles. An old bank ledger book which she used as a writing journal contains notes for thirty-two articles including: a tribute to Rachael Jackson, wife of President Jackson; the story of Margaret of Parma, Regent of the Netherlands in 1559, a woman of great ability who was forced to resign; the differences between the brains of men and women; and the writing of Jean Paul Marat, who contributed the idea of meritocracy to the French Revolution.[22]

She published an article about one of her favorite historical figures, Catherine II, czarina of Russia. She wrote that "during her reign of thirty-three years, her dominions were increased nearly one-twentieth, and one-third in population. As early as 6 o'clock every morning, she was in her cabinet opening dispatches and issuing orders to her generals and deciding on petitions. She never exacted Asiatic servility from her people and never [concerned] herself about trifles. She abolished torture and exempted nobles, also burghers from corporal punishment—honor to whom honor is due."[23]

Her last book, *Sport of Kings: Racing Stories*, dedicated to "Lovers of the Thoroughbred Horse," was published by Broadway Press, New York in 1912. The book contains short stories that embody turf lore and knowledge gained through her experience in breeding and racing Thoroughbreds. Sport of Kings is the most widely available of her books and is included in many libraries and private collections of Thoroughbred racing stories.[24]

She began to research family history. In December 1912 she wrote to a Russell cousin, Carter H. Harrison IV, Mayor of Chicago, to try to locate a portrait of her great grandfather, Brig. Gen. William Russell of Virginia, but she was unsuccessful.[25]

Another cousin, Maitland Allen of Warren County, Virginia had collected several of her father's letters to his family, and he sent Colonel Russell's letters to her.[26] She also obtained from Anna des Cognets in Lexington her father's letters to his brother, Thomas A. Russell. Based upon her research, she prepared an article for the *Lexington Herald*, "Two Old Russell Homes on the Russell Road," which was published on November 28, 1915.

One of Josephine's most prized possession was the old battle flag of Col. Eugene Erwin's regiment—the Sixth Missouri Infantry CSA. Josephine had transported the flag and Eugene's uniform hidden under her dress from Vicksburg to Independence, Missouri. The material for the flag was

Fig. 8.4 Battle Flag of the Sixth Missouri Infantry CSA. *Wood Simpson*

imported crimson merino from England, hand sewn in Richmond, Virginia. It has a buff fringe on its border and a field of thirteen yellow stars with a new moon in the upper-left corner. At Eugene Erwin's request, Josephine sewed an inscription with the regiment's designation on the flag shortly after the Battle of Corinth, Mississippi. Ensign William Huff carried the flag in the Corinth assault and was shot nine times before he fell on the flag, drenching the stars with his blood. Over 70 percent of the Sixth Missouri unit was killed or wounded at Corinth, and to the survivors, the flag became a symbol of their fallen comrades. Over the years, Josephine sent the flag to reunions of the regiment in Missouri. The meetings opened with the unfurling of the flag and the reading of a letter from Josephine Erwin Clay by a surviving officer. In 1885, Maj. E. A. Hickman, who had accompanied Josephine on her return from Vicksburg, read her letter "asking the survivors to show it to their children, a relic made sacred by its baptism in the fire and smoke of battle. I feel happy in being instrumental in its preservation . . . ." Twenty-three out of the one hundred living survivors of the unit, which had once numbered six hundred men, attended. When the flag was sent back to Lexington, it arrived in the evening at the Lexington Express office. During the night, a fire broke out in the building, and a man ran into the building to save as many letters as he could, but he emerged with only one package—it proved to be the flag.[27]

On June 13, 1913, Josephine sent the flag for the last time to a reunion of over 15,000 Federal and Confederate survivors at Higginsville, Missouri. The program began with a moment of silence to honor the dead, then the crowd let out a mighty roar as the flag was unfurled.[28]

For the first time, Josephine Clay took an interest in school athletics by following the career of her grandson, Henry Clay Simpson, who played basketball and football at the University of Kentucky. During his third year, he joined many of his fellow players and volunteered for the armed forces as the U.S. entered World War I.

After the armistice, Josephine received a letter from Victor Bogaret, the local director of the Belgian War Relief, thanking her for seventy-five pairs of knitted socks that were sent to the children of soldiers killed in the World War.[29] "Words, either spoken or written, utterly fail to express my deep appreciation of your noble gift to the soldiers of my native land Belgium . . . I sincerely trust you will be spared for many years to come to the world, which has become a better place for your having lived." One pair was displayed in the national museum in Brussels. This recalled her gift of seventy-five pairs of knitted socks sent almost sixty years earlier to the Confederate soldiers in Mississippi.

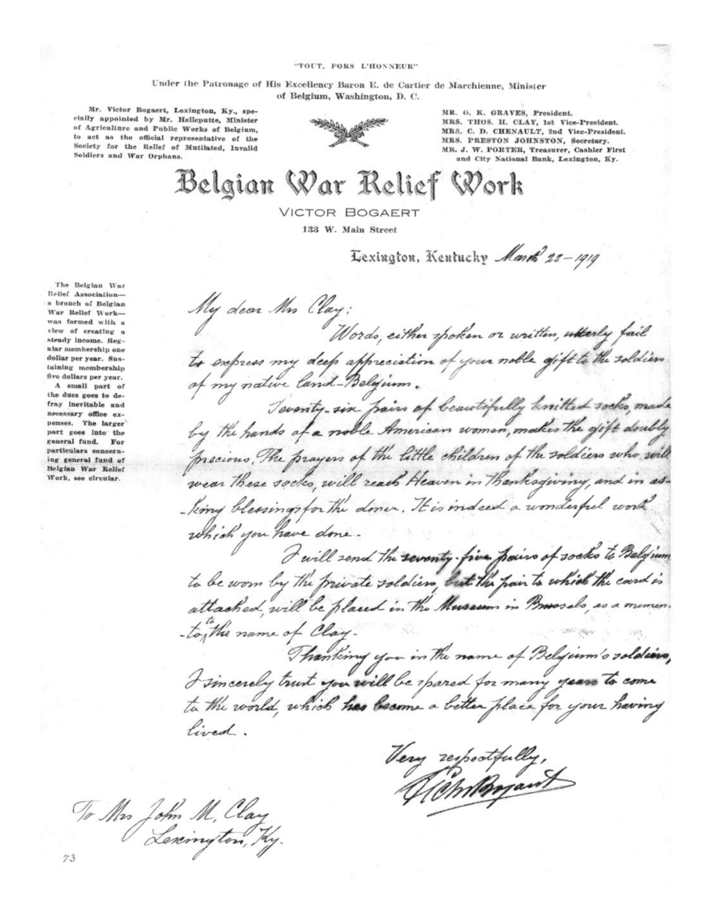

"TOUT, FORS L'HONNEUR"

Under the Patronage of His Excellency Baron E. de Cartier de Marchienne, Minister of Belgium, Washington, D. C.

Mr. Victor Bogaert, Lexington, Ky., specially appointed by Mr. Helleputte, Minister of Agriculture and Public Works of Belgium, to act as the official representative of the Society for the Relief of Mutilated, Invalid Soldiers and War Orphans.

MR. G. K. GRAVES, President.
MRS. THOS. H. CLAY, 1st Vice-President.
MRS. C. D. CHENAULT, 2nd Vice-President.
MRS. PRESTON JOHNSTON, Secretary.
MR. J. W. PORTER, Treasurer, Cashier First and City National Bank, Lexington, Ky.

Belgian War Relief Work

VICTOR BOGAERT

133 W. Main Street

The Belgian War Relief Association—a branch of Belgian War Relief Work—was formed with a view of creating a steady income. Regular membership one dollar per year. Sustaining membership five dollars per year.

A small part of the dues goes to defray inevitable and necessary office expenses. The larger part goes into the general fund. For particulars concerning general fund of Belgian War Relief Work, see circular.

Lexington, Kentucky March 22–1919

My dear Mrs Clay:

Words, either spoken or written, utterly fail to express my deep appreciation of your noble gift to the soldiers of my native land-Belgium.

Seventy-six pairs of beautifully knitted socks, made by the hands of a noble American woman, makes the gift doubly precious. The prayers of the little children of the soldiers who will wear these socks, will reach Heaven in Thanksgiving, and in asking blessings for the donor. It is indeed a wonderful work which you have done.

I will send the seventy-five pairs of socks to Belgium to be worn by the private soldiers, but the pair to which the card is attached, will be placed in the Museum in Brussels, as a memento to the name of Clay.

Thanking you in the name of Belgium's soldiers, I sincerely trust you will be spared for many years to come to the world, which has become a better place for your having lived.

Very respectfully,
V. Bogaert

To Mrs John M. Clay
Lexington, Ky.

73

Fig. 8.7 Victor Bogaret to Josephine Clay, March 22, 1919

After recovering from an illness over the winter of 1920, Josephine baked a cake to help celebrate the birthday of Dr. James K. Patterson, the first president of the University of Kentucky. Dr. Patterson was a close family friend, married to Lucelia Wing, a Russell cousin.[30] After his birthday celebration, Dr. Patterson wrote:

> Mrs. John M. Clay   Ashland   Lexington, Kentucky
>
> My dear kinswoman,
>
> My birthday has caused so many expressions and manifestations of regard from my friends that I feel abashed and amazed. No greeting, however, came to me with more affection than did the one from you and none came which I value more. The cake is a work of art and is very delicious. I thank you for it.

> Our birthdays are coming now with ominous frequency. I hope that you are recovering and are being refreshed and re-invigorated by your change. I shall endeavor to call to see you some time in the near future, and I should value a visit from you at any time.
>
> Sincerely and affectionately yours,
> James K. Patterson[31]

She did not receive his letter. The day after the letter was written, on Monday, March 29, 1920, Josephine Clay died at her home at the age of eighty-four.

Josephine Clay grew up on the Missouri frontier in a large family (with six brothers) dominated by a father who loved adventure and travel but who struggled to live up to the expectations of his family. She accompanied her father, who called her "Joe," on various trips in the early American West and loved his sense of adventure. When her marriage brought her into the Civil War conflict and Grant's siege at Vicksburg, the result was disastrous for her family. After a difficult period, she adopted an independent approach to life, unusual for a woman at that time, but it foretold a unique career. Her second marriage brought her to Kentucky, and after her husband died, to the management of a well known bluegrass horse farm. Her acceptance of this role, her hard work and attention to detail led to a pioneering success. While she became an advocate of career opportunities for other women in her novels and by example, she was not a revolutionary or an active member of the women's movement. She created opportunities for many women that followed with careers in the Thoroughbred horse business.

Despite her pioneering success in horse breeding, she has been largely forgotten today. In Lyman Weeks' history of horse racing, her tenure at Ashland was described as follows:

> After the death of Mr. Clay, his widow succeeded to the head of the establishment and for years was the only woman in the United States engaged in this particular kind of business. She had a complete knowledge of the blood horse and of breeding methods, while the pedigrees of all the great Thoroughbreds were as household words to her. She was not less successful than her husband had been in raising some distinguished performers for the turf and in adding value to the blood of the American race horse.[32]

Josephine often used her husband's name in writing about the Ashland Stock Farm, and this may have encouraged equine historians to recognize her success as an extension of her husband. It is time to recognize Josephine Clay's contribution in her own right.

An article about her death appeared in the *Lexington Herald:*

> In the passing of Mrs. Clay, Lexington loses perhaps the most remarkable woman of her generation, a writer of prose and poetry, a successful business woman, fearless and intrepid in spirit, brilliant in mind and admired for beauty, wit and all the womanly graces as well. She was engaged in activities which won for her national fame, having been the world's most noted and successful woman owner and breeder of fine Thoroughbred horses.[33]

Epilogue

Private funeral services were held for Josephine Clay at Christ Church Cathedral with the Very Rev. Robert K. Massie, Dean, officiating. She was buried next to John M. Clay at the Lexington Cemetery. In 1888, she had purchased a 1,495-square foot lot adjacent to John M. Clay's monument with space to bury her descendants. Over the years, she had arranged for several members of the Clay family to be buried in her lot. She commissioned a memorial stone dedicated to her first husband, Col. Eugene Erwin; and in 1894, arranged for his remains to be cremated and moved from Vicksburg and buried under the stone she dedicated to him. The remains of Eugene Erwin's mother, Anne Clay Erwin, were moved to her lot from another location in the Lexington Cemetery. She also moved to her lot the remains of her daughter, Nettie E. Gratz, from the old Episcopal Cemetery on Third Street in Lexington and Henry Clay's twelve-year-old daughter, Eliza H. Clay, from Ohio.[1] Josephine's daughters agreed that the Anderson grandchildren were to be buried on one side of the John M. Clay monument and the Simpson grandchildren on the other side.[2]

Josephine's will was handwritten, dated October 31, 1910. All of her property was left to her two living daughters, Lucretia Erwin Simpson and Mary Erwin Anderson. The real estate, however, was subject to the following conditions: "It shall be managed by my two daughters without the control or interference of any husband they now have or may have and the emoluments to be divided equally between the two, but should not be sold until the death of my last surviving daughter; then it is to be divided between my daughters' children to share alike .... It is my earnest wish that the future heirs may so arrange that Ashland may not pass out of the possession of my descendants. I repeat that there shall be no sale of the land until it becomes subject to division among the heirs as set forth above." A codicil added two years later permitted the sale of land she owned in Missouri and specified that Henry Clay's gold watch was to be given to her grandson, Henry Clay Simpson.[3] The value of the estate was estimated by the Lexington Herald to be over $200,000.[4] At the time of her death, the Ashland horse farm property she inherited had grown to 412 acres on the southeastern outskirts of the growing city of Lexington.[5] In addition, she owned over 500 acres farther out the Tates Creek Road and a downtown office building.

What could Josephine have been thinking about when she excluded her daughters' spouses from the management of her property? Perhaps she was concerned about the Erwin family experience and the possibility that a present or future spouse of her daughters would encumber the property with debt.

Problems continued to plague the settlement of James Erwin's estate. On June 24, 1918, a court action was filed in Caddo Parish in Louisiana on behalf of the heirs of James Erwin claiming property owned by his estate near Shreveport, Louisiana.[6] Despite over half a century of legal action and a file of correspondence inches thick, there is no record of land being recovered for the Erwin estate.

When Lucretia Erwin Simpson died in 1929 at the age of seventy-five and Mary Erwin Anderson died in 1931 at the age of seventy, the surviving grandchildren, the Simpsons (Josephine, Eugene and Henry Clay) and Andersons (Henry Clay and Mathew William), had the acres surveyed and divided into five lots. They determined the ownership of the lots by drawing slips of paper from a hat. Henry Clay Anderson, who received most of the Pettit farm, sold his share to John F. White, a wealthy

Table 2. Property Acquired in Central Kentucky by Josephine Clay
Search of Deeds Recorded by Josephine Clay in Fayette County by William A. LaBach

Date	Description	How Acquired	Disposition
1887	**Henry Clay Estate** 248 acres which includes a 200-acre portion of Henry Clay estate and 48 acres purchased by John M. Clay. Ashland Park to Tates Creek Pike.	Inherited from John M. Clay	In 1934, 9.66 acres were sold to Board of Education for Cassidy and Morton Schools. Other properties were incorporated into the Chevy Chase Subdivision and sold by the heirs of Josephine Clay as lots for apartment houses and homes beginning in the 1940s.
1898	**Armstrong Mill Road Farm** 250 acres on the Armstrong Mill Road, Lexington	The initial property was purchased from Lydia B. Todhunter with contiguous parcels purchased in 1903 and 1911.	Sold by the heirs of Josephine Clay.
1898	**Minor Simpson Farm and Surrounding property** Property totaling over 600 acres on Tates Creek, Walnut Hill, East Hickman and Delong Roads in Fayette County.	The initial purchase in 1898 was a half interest in 370 acres from her son-in-law, Minor Simpson, for $9,000. Nearby parcels on East Hickman Creek and Delong Road were purchased in 1901, 1902 and 1912.	Sold 179 acres to William J. Baxter in 1920. In 1931, the heirs of Josephine Clay sold 267 acres to John B. and Marshall Johnson and in 1933 sold 183 acres to Brownell and Mary Sayre Combs.
1899	**Downtown House** 87.5 feet frontage on the north side of East Main Street between Walnut and Deweese Streets, a double brick dwelling house in Lexington.	Purchased from Northern Bank for $4,500.	Sold in 1911 to Jennie W. Smith for $6,500.
1899	**Downtown Office Property** 77.5 feet frontage on the southwest corner of Market and Church Streets in Lexington.	Purchased from Northern Bank	A two story office building constructed on the property at a later date was sold by her grandson, Henry Clay Simpson, in 1980.
1904	**Downtown House** 70 front feet on North Upper between Church and Market Streets.	Purchased from the Second Presbyterian Church.	Sold to C. M. Marshall in 1912.
1909	**Lakewood Section of Chevy Chase** 175-acre Pettit farm and Harmony Hall on the Mount Tabor Road in Fayette County.	Purchased from G. Nat Pettit for $15,970.	The property was developed in lots by John F. White and Henry Clay Simpson in cooperation with Jack W. Davis and other builders beginning in the 1950s.

Fig. 9.1 Henry Clay Simpson and his mother, Lucretia Erwin Simpson, with the Ice Houses of Ashland in the Background

local businessman. This property included a large house, Harmony Hall, which White renovated and lived in for a number of years.[7]

Ashland on Tates Creek Road was rented and a dairy operated by the Nash family on the property until the 1950s, when the house was sold to the Chevy Chase Baptist Church. The house was torn down and replaced by the church at 200 Colony Boulevard. Mathew William Anderson, Jr., who owned the surrounding property, developed a series of apartment complexes. Josephine Clay's land farther out the Tates Creek Road was sold in the 1930s for the development of horse farms, with one parcel now comprising Overbrook, founded by the late W. T. Young.

Beginning in 1953, my father, acting on behalf of his older brother and sister, subdivided the parcel of land that the Simpson family inherited. Over the first two years of the development, they sold forty-eight lots and reported capital gains for the money received on the sales. The Internal Revenue Service ruled that sales were made in the course of conducting a real estate business and the gains were taxable as ordinary income. The Simpson heirs went to court to challenge the ruling and the case was tried on June 8, 1959 in Louisville, Kentucky before U. S. Tax Court Judge J. Gregory Bruce from Pineville, Kentucky.

The attorney for the Simpson family, William Bagby from Lexington, described what happened in the court room.

> I had [the three Simpsons] sit beside me at the counsel table. The case was called by the court clerk and then, during my opening statement, I had each rise to be introduced to

> Judge Bruce as direct descendants of Henry Clay; and they each rose and gave a brief bow. Judge Bruce, most gentlemanly, rose slightly from his chair and gave a smiling bow.
>
> A copy of the original, revered will of Henry Clay was introduced into evidence revealing his disposal of the land. This was followed by evidence of the generation steps of the land inherited by the Simpson heirs.
>
> Miss Josephine Clay Simpson who was 80 (and partially blind), Mr. Eugene Simpson who was 79 (and partially deaf) and Henry Clay Simpson, 63 (and recovered from a lengthy stay in a sanitarium for tuberculosis), testified . . . in detail about the handling of the sale of the land and said the sole and only purpose was to liquidate the inherited farm land—convert it to cash and that when this land was all liquidated the Simpson Realty Company would end.[8]
>
> Judge Bruce in his Opinion, filed weeks after the trial, ruled that the facts revealed that the Henry Clay heirs had no intention of going into business but that their sole purpose was to liquidate the inherited land at a fair price and, therefore, the gains were not taxable as ordinary income but as capital gains.

Bagby described this case as: "The great Henry Clay 'Arises' to Defeat the IRS for his Kentucky Heirs."[9]

Over the years until his death in 1986 at the age of ninety, my father continued to develop a successful subdivision of his grandmother's property with distinctive road plans that preserved many old trees from the horse farm and more diversity in the size and style of houses and apartments than can be found in many other areas of Lexington. This subdivision, Chevy Chase, was named after a golf club in Maryland that he joined while working in Washington, D. C. in the 1920s.[10]

My aunt, Josephine Clay Simpson, followed her mother by becoming a lifelong member of The Woman's Club of Central Kentucky, which advocated an active role for women in public affairs.[11] She lived until her death on Market Street in Gratz Park in Lexington. Across the park was the former home of Gen. John Hunt Morgan, now a museum. She insisted that she never visited the house to protest Morgan's theft of horses from Ashland. My uncle, Eugene Erwin Simpson, became a professor of civil engineering at Lafayette College and retired to live in Lexington. His widow, Marguerite G. Simpson died in 1979 and left her estate to establish a fund, administered by the University of Kentucky, to support the Donovan Scholar program underwriting the cost of seniors returning to university classes.[12]

All that remains today of Josephine Clay's horse farm that once comprised over four hundred acres and included twenty-five miles of plank fences, twenty-six buildings, thirty gates, and two one-mile training tracks, are a few old ash, chestnut, and sycamore trees that surrounded the Ashland training tracks. The location of the tracks can be detected from the air by a pattern of trees, but there is no trace of the tracks on the ground. The entrance to the tracks was behind the house once owned by the late Adolph Rupp, University of Kentucky basketball coach on Eastover Drive.[13] The large horse barn, located near the Catholic church and school, Christ the King was torn down by the Nash family. The only property still owned by the descendents of Josephine Clay is a section of the Romany Road shopping center which was leased on a long-term basis to store owners in the 1950s.

The population of the Lexington metropolitan area now exceeds 400,000, and the town's development extends five miles beyond John and Josephine Clay's home on the Tates Creek Road. The

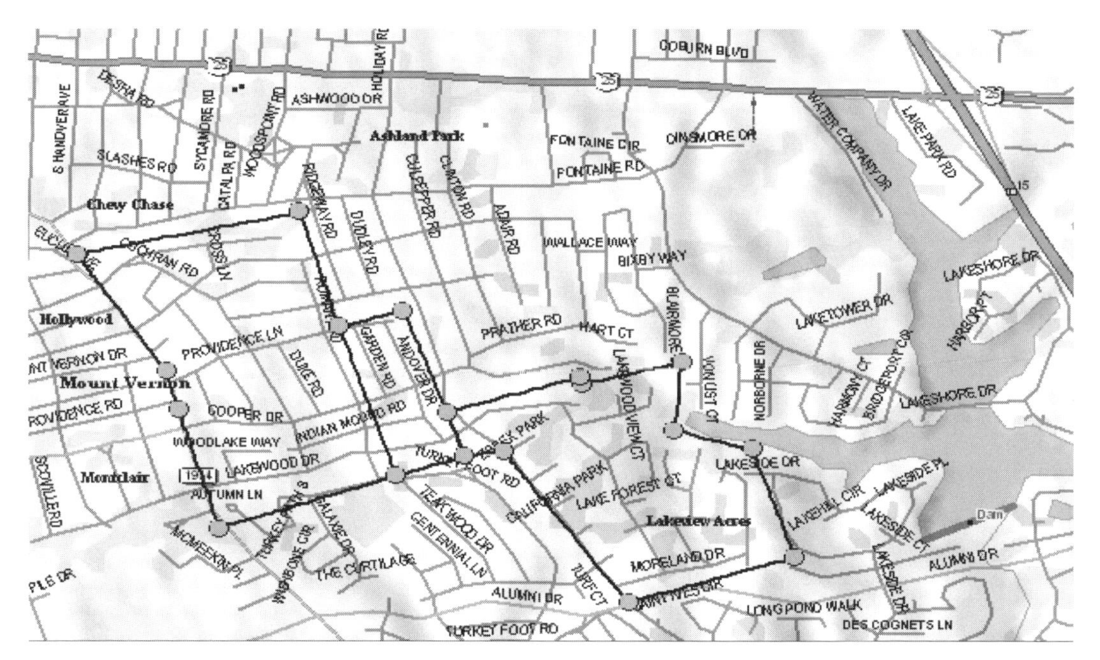

9.2 Map of Chevy Chase, Lexington, Kentucky showing the location of Ashland Stock Farm (left), the additional acreage purchased by John M. Clay (middle) and the Pettit Farm purchased by Josephine Clay (right). Prepared by William A. LaBach[14]

breeding of Thoroughbred horses in the United States is centered in the bluegrass area, where there are 460 Thoroughbred horse farms providing employment directly and indirectly to 52,000 people, generating $1.2 billion in annual horse sales.[15] Ashland, the home of Henry and Lucretia Clay, rebuilt by James Clay in 1857, is now preserved as a museum and National Historic Landmark along with fourteen acres of the original Henry Clay estate.

The legacy of Ashland Stock Farm continues in the bloodlines of Thoroughbred horses. Research by Cathy C. Schenck at the Keeneland Association Library identified twenty winners of Triple Crown races (the Kentucky Derby, Preakness, or Belmont) descended from Henry Clay's two foundation broodmares, *Magnolia* and *Margaret Wood*. The following Kentucky Derby winners were part of Ashland's legacy:

Tracing to *Magnolia*:

Day Star 1878
Lawrin 1938
Middleground 1950
Venetian Way 1960
Sunny's Halo 1983

Tracing to *Margaret Wood:*

Riley 1890
Azra 1892
Ben Brush 1896

Regret 1915
Exterminator 1918
Gato del Sol 1982

Descendents of *Margaret Wood* standing today include *Gato Del Sol*, now retired at Stone Farm; *Yes It's True* at Three Chimneys Farm; *Will's Way* at Brookdale Farm; and *Thunder Rumble* in New York.[16]

Anne Peters, the pedigree expert at Robert N. Clay's Three Chimneys Farm, studied the progeny of *Magnolia* and prepared a list of standing stallions descended from *Magnolia*. Nearly all were traced through the famous broodmare, *Maggie B. B.* In the bluegrass, the following stallions were identified:

Dixieland Band – Lane's End Farm
Dixie Union – Lane's End Farm
Unbridled's Song – Taylor Made Farm
Cryptoclearance – Margaux Farm
Malabar Gold – Highclere Farm
Rod and Staff – Old Frankfort Stud
Zavata – Walmac Farm
Harlan's Holiday – Airdrie Stud Farm
Cozzene – Gainesway Farm

There are twenty-two standing stallions traced to *Magnolia* at other locations in the United States and Canada, and thirteen stallions standing overseas in eight countries.

Peters' research found that the *Magnolia* female line on occasion produced stallions that are oddly marked. *Airdrie Apache* at Painted Desert Farm in Oregon is a spotted Thoroughbred and has sired a pure white offspring. *Puchilingui* is a speckled roan horse, and *Kentucky Colonel* sired *White Beauty,* the famous pure white filly.[17]

Chronology of the Life of Josephine Russell Erwin Clay

1802	William Henry Russell is born at "Poplar Hill," on the Russell Cave Road north of Lexington, one of the Russell homes on a 2,000-acre land grant from Gov. Thomas Jefferson of Virginia.
1824	Russell marries Miss Zaenett Freeland in Calvert County, Maryland.
1831	He becomes acquainted with Henry Clay at Transylvania College and serves as clerk in his law office in Lexington. After graduation, Russell practices law in Nicholas County, where he was elected to the Kentucky legislature. He claims to be instrumental in the election of Henry Clay to the U.S. Senate.
	The Russell family moves to a community near Fulton, Missouri, sixty miles from St. Louis.
1832	Russell is appointed colonel of the Missouri militia and leads a fighting force in the Seminole Indian Wars in Florida.
December 7, 1835	Josephine Deborah Russell is born at the family home in Missouri. She was the fifth child and only daughter among the seven children of William and Zaenett Russell.
1838–1841	Russell serves in the Missouri legislature during this period.
1841	With Henry Clay's assistance, Col. William H. Russell is appointed U. S. marshal for Missouri and the Kansas/Nebraska/Iowa Indian territories.
May 1843	Russell is informed by President John Tyler in a meeting in Washington, D. C., that he was to be replaced as U. S. marshal.
June 1843	The Russell family visits Ashland, home of Henry Clay, and Colonel Russell offers assistance in Clay's bid for the presidential nomination.
1844	Henry Clay is defeated in the presidential election by James K. Polk.
1846	To investigate career opportunities in California, Colonel Russell joins a large wagon train to California that includes the Donner Party. He serves as Captain during the early part of the crossing.
	Zaenett Russell writes a letter to her brother-in-law, Thomas Russell, telling him that she can no longer afford Josephine Russell's private tutor. Josephine begins reading great literature and is called a "bluestocking."
	Col. Russell joins a military force sponsored by the U. S. government called the "California Battalion" as ordnance officer. Under the leadership of U. S. Army Col. John C. Frémont, they accept the surrender of the Mexicans of Alta California.
1847	Frémont is appointed acting governor of the California territories and Russell is appointed secretary of state.
	Frémont is replaced by U. S. Army General Stephen Kearney, recalled to Washington, D. C., and charged with mutiny. Russell returns east via the Santa Fe Trail to testify on behalf of Frémont. The caravan led by Russell is attacked three times by Indians on the trail.
1848	Frémont is convicted, but President Polk dismisses the charge of mutiny and remits the sentences.

Russell serves as a delegate supporting Henry Clay at the Whig Presidential nominating convention in Philadelphia. He leaves the convention when it becomes apparent that Gen. Zachary Taylor will be nominated.

1849 — Russell, his wife Zaenett, and his children Josephine, Henry Clay, and George Washington join a Gold Rush wagon train to San Francisco, where Russell plans to attend the California Constitutional Convention. Josephine is thirteen at the time.

1850 — Eugene Erwin, grandson of Henry Clay, is hired by the Pacific Mail Steamship Co. in New York and assigned to keep the books at the company's office in Monterey, California.

1851 — Russell is appointed Collector of Customs at Monterey, CA.

The Russell family travels to Mexico City. Josephine's father asks her to keep a journal on the trip and her writing career begins.

James Erwin, father of Eugene Erwin, dies in Lexington. Eugene Erwin later receives a $10,000 share of the proceeds of the sale of the family home, the "Woodlands," in Lexington.

1852 — Henry Clay dies in Washington, D.C., and leaves his son John 200 acres and a one-half interest in valuable Thoroughbred horses. His wife Lucretia gives the other half-interest in the horses to her son.

1853 — Josephine Russell and Eugene Erwin, accompanied by Colonel Russell, return to Missouri to be married. They travel to Nicaragua on the steamship *SS Sierra Nevada* owned by Commodore Cornelius Vanderbilt. After visiting Lexington, the couple marry in July 1853 in Callaway County, Missouri.

1853 — Mr. and Mrs. Eugene Erwin move to Independence, Missouri, where Eugene joins a mercantile business and continues to pursue the land claims of his father's estate.

Four daughters are born to the Erwin family: Lucretia Clay "Lula" in 1854, Zaenett "Nettie" in 1857, Mary Webster "Mamie" in 1861, and Eugenia who survives only a few days in 1864.

1861 — Eugene Erwin volunteers for the Missouri State Guards and then resigns and joins the Confederate Infantry in Missouri. He is sent to Arkansas and Mississippi to fight Federal forces in the area of Vicksburg.

1862 — Eugene Erwin is promoted to Colonel in charge of the Sixth Missouri Infantry Regiment.

1863 — In response to pressure on Confederate wives in Independence, Josephine travels by wagon through the Union lines to Grand Gulf, Mississippi, to rejoin her husband, accompanied by her nine-year-old daughter Lula.

After several failures attacking the Confederate positions in Vicksburg, Gen. Ulysses S. Grant with a force of 70,000 troops begins a siege of Vicksburg that lasts six weeks.

June 25, 1863 — Union soldiers attack Fort Hill on the main road to Vicksburg. In leading a counter attack, Eugene Erwin is killed instantly by a gunshot to the heart. He is buried near Stouts Bayou by his men. His uniform and the Sixth Missouri battle flag are presented to Josephine Erwin.

July 3, 1863 — Gen. John C. Pemberton CSA meets with General Grant and asks for terms. The Vicksburg campaign is over on July 4.

Josephine and Lula meet with General Grant at his Vicksburg headquarters at Lum House on Washington Street. The General writes out two passes—one for "Mrs. Col.

	Erwin and family to go to Missouri passage free on any government vessel" and another pass for Lieutenant Hickman to accompany them to Cairo, Ill, and to return on the first vessel for parole.
	Lieutenant Hickman, Josephine and Lula board the Army transport Imperial and travel to Cairo and St. Louis as authorized. Josephine and Lula return to Independence, MO.
Christmas, 1863	Josephine Erwin receives a letter from "Uncle" John Clay.
1864	She gives birth to Eugenia, named for her fallen husband, but the baby lives only a few days.
	One of John Clay's best race horses—*Skedaddle*—is stolen by the men of Confederate raider Gen. John Hunt Morgan camping near Ashland. John M. Clay rides after the troop to Georgetown and confronts General Morgan. John Clay pays $900 for his own horses.
July 7, 1866	Josephine Erwin marries John Clay in Lexington. She has married a son and a grandson of Henry Clay.
	She becomes actively involved in managing the Ashland Stock Farm while Clay travels to racetracks in the East.
1873	Josephine Clay publishes *What Will the World Say? and Only a Woman* using a pseudonym, Ojos Morenos (Dark Eyes).
	Josephine Clay becomes a grandmother when John Morrison Simpson is born. He is the son of Lucretia Erwin and her husband Minor Simpson, a local farmer. Her other grandchildren are Josephine Clay Simpson, born in 1878, Eugene Erwin Simpson in 1880, Henry Clay Anderson in 1891, George Anderson in 1893, Matthew William Anderson, Jr. in 1895, and Henry Clay Simpson in 1896. The Anderson grandchildren are the sons of daughter Mary Anderson, who married banker Matthew William Anderson of Independence, Missouri.
August 10, 1887	John M. Clay dies and Josephine inherits Ashland on Tates Creek Pike and twelve brood mares, all descendants of Henry Clay's famous broodmares *Magnolia* and *Margaret Wood.*
	Josephine Clay publishes her second novel *Some Little Angels Still Left.*
1888	Josephine Clay announces that she will own and manage Ashland Stock Farm.
	The Henry Clay racing colors of Buff and Blue are reregistered by Josephine Clay.
1900	Josephine Clay's horse operation is very successful, and she builds her stock to over fifty brood mares and two stallions. An article in a New York newspaper reports that she is often seen riding across her farm wearing a broad-brimmed straw hat, carrying her Colt pistol, and talking to her horses.
	She invests the proceeds of horse sales in farm property farther out the Tates Creek Pike, downtown real estate, and improvements to her horse farm.
1899	*Uncle Phil* is published, Josephine Clay's most successful novel.
1901	The novel *Frank Logan* is published.
1903	Although Josephine Clay was unable to attend, her paper "Women in the Professions" is presented at the International Conference of Women in Toronto, Canada, and is reprinted by several newspapers.

	The Minor Simpson family moves to Ashland on Tate Creek Pike and assists Josephine Clay in managing her farm.
	A dispersal sale for Ashland Stock Farm is held with disappointing results.
1909	Josephine Clay purchases the Pettit Farm, adding 175 acres to Ashland on Tates Creek Pike.
1910	After Josephine Clay breaks her hip, she lives most of the time in her suite of rooms on the first floor of her home but continues to research and write articles and books.
1912	*The Sport of Kings,* a book of Josephine Clay's racing stories, is published.
1919	Josephine receives a letter from Victor Bogaret, local Director of the Belgian War Relief, thanking her for seventy-five pairs of knitted socks which were sent to the children of soldiers of the World War.
March 29, 1920	Josephine Clay dies, age 85, at her home, and is buried next to John M. Clay at the Lexington Cemetery.
1929	Lucretia Simpson dies.
1931	Mary Anderson dies, permitting Josephine Clay's property in Lexington to be distributed to her grandchildren. Ashland on Tates Creek Pike and the Pettit Farm are subsequently incorporated into a new subdivision of Lexington, Chevy Chase.

Selections from the Writing of Josephine Clay

a. Who Rode La Sylphide?[1]

The Sport of Kings: Racing Stories (New York, 1912)
A story of the Lexington Race Course
Respectfully inscribed to
Lovers of the Thoroughbred Horse
The only true aristocrats

Near the Phoenix Hotel, more than twenty years ago, two men chanced to meet. They were "Old Sports," so designated; for while disconnected with the respectable, legitimate turf, they earned a precarious livelihood by doing business on betting lines—not always commendable—incidental to turf matters, but perhaps no other calling fixes its impression with such unerring certainty.

It is not the gorgeous waistcoat and flashy necktie emblazoned with a golden horse shoe. Nor is it the gleaming diamond on the left-hand, fourth finger, so much as the facial expression engendered by constantly recurring alternations of intensified hopes and fears—the elation with winning, and the dejection of losing.

They shook hands, and reciprocally asked: "How are times?" Fortune had been kind to both, and they said so, but the inmost soul of each man was burdened with a tormenting mystery. With a single exception, there had been no turf secret that they had not been able to probe to the depths. This exception was the occasion of humiliating sorrow, and indicated, as they feared, failing powers—hence, the anxious enquiry: "Has it been found out yet who rode La Sylphide?"

The answer was delivered slowly, reluctantly:

"Not for dead certain; but there is some that suspect it might have been a woman."

"Weren't no woman. I saw him close when old Mat fetched him out of the weighin room. He was black and a puny chap, and looked half-dead. I had smart money on the mare, and she being a difficult mount, I had my mind on her jock. So me and some other fellows tried to crowd in to get near enough to size him up, but old Mat let fly at us with the worst language I ever heard—he's got a mighty rough tongue; and what surprised me was the sugary way he spoke to that boy—so ornery looking too—and cheerfully lifted him up to the saddle."

The exceeding beauty of a Kentucky stock farm cannot be adequately described when the trees are in the graceful foliage of early summer, the glowing sun, in generous profusion, pouring down the warmth of golden light all over the living sheen of the luxuriant blue-grass. And beneath the azure sky, fresh and fragrant are the breezes that waft over the sweetest flowers. The butterflies dance and glance, making a gleam of tangled colors as they come and go, flashing hither and yon, or settling to feed on the rich hearts of blooming plants.

Within the ten counties distinctively called the "Blue Grass Region," there was no lovelier estate than the one over which Jack Chetwyn is conducting his blue-eyed, new wife toward the training stable to exhibit to her, as he proudly said: "The most beautiful creature on earth—save only you ma mie." Assured of the sympathy from his new partner, he continued: "With the paternal acres I inherited the race stock, and have always had my fair share of fliers, and I have one now that leads them all. But she has the drawback of an uncontrollable temper, and she is full of such freakouts as are past finding out. And she has in her time caused bitter sorrow to many a gallant plunger; though all the while when we were in New York, so gaily fluttering away our honeymoon, I had repeated letters from my trainer saying that she had turned over a new leaf, and was doing as well as he could wish. So well that he had entered her in a mile-and-quarter handicap, and had backed her for every cent he could raise. As a rule, I do not bet on my horses, but catching the infection from Davis, who is rarely over-sanguine, I sent a large commission, and, "dear"—he continued rather sheepishly—"that's not all—I did so want to buy for you that lot of diamonds you admired at Tiffanys—but the price was too steep for my means. However, the great news about the mare so exhilarated me that I gave my IOU."

"Oh, Jack," she said reproachfully, and almost in tears, "I really did not care for the diamonds so very much, and if I did, it was only a passing fancy. Now should the mare not win, I shall feel like a horrid wretch."

"Don't worry, dear; La Sylphide—is not that a pretty name?—will certainly win." His tone carried conviction, and she felt reassured; she believed in Jack. And it seemed to her that his admission about the diamonds was very magnanimous, and then and there she resolved to be on even terms with him in open-heartedness. She too would make a confession:

"Jackey," she said deprecatingly, "don't be shocked, but once upon a time I was a terrible tomboy. When I left school I was delicate, had a cough, and papa sent me down to Uncle Ben's cattle ranch in Texas, where I stayed a whole year and learned to ride. I took to horses, and horses took to me—I have broken many a colt no one else could do anything with. And many a race I have won over the prairies with my cousins—and beat them—the horses would run freer for me. Uncle Ben often said of me and my mount that we did not seem a pair, only just one embodiment. There was such unity and friendship. You do not understand."

"I do understand," he answered; "there never was a time when I was not fond of a good horse. A good horse I regard with profound admiration. Many of his traits tally closely with the best traits of the noblest human; faithful, loving, courageous—even when writhing under an injury so ready to forgive. For a kind word he will put forth his best efforts. And forsaking his kind he will give all, willing to labor, to suffer, to die." Suddenly the panegyric ceased. "Ha yi! What's going on?"

Jack Chetwyn's blood almost froze in his veins seeing what he saw. A beautiful bay mare, held with difficulty by two stout stablemen, was prancing, kicking, wheeling, jumping, backing, in short performing, apparently simultaneously, every action within the compass of violently energized and tremendous muscularity. Mr. Mat Davis, the trainer, who was standing near, his countenance faithfully portraying combined anger, horror and despair. These emotions were quickly communicated to the face of Mr. Chetwyn as he rapidly arrived at the scene.

"What's the matter, Davis?" he asked. "What ails the mare?"

Old Mat, with great presence of mind—he had pride in his manners—bowed to the lady, whose fleetness of foot rivaled her husband, before answering gloomily: "In my opinion, it's a case of all-possessed, gone loony all of a sudden. She has been kind as a suckin' dove—the littlest boy in the stable could exercise her. But just now she comes out of her stall in such a fury as never was, and she throwed boy after boy as fast as we could fling them into the saddle. This stable is turned into a hospital. There ain't a sound rider left." This melancholy statement receives confirmation: groans and lamentations coming from some half-dozen small-sized humans scattered around in various stages of ruin. "And what are we going to do—the races not three weeks off—I don't know. But it all could be rectified if that blasted mare—I beg your pardon, mum—hadn't throwed us over. We had such good prospects! We stood to win a fearful pile of money. Now, everything has gone to blue smash. If steamboats were sellin' for ten cents apiece we couldn't collectively, buy a yawl. And worse yet—Oh, Daniel the Prophet! there's my sister that I persuaded, I felt so sure of that infernal mare—I beg your pardon, mum—to take the long odds with that hard cash she had saved up to pay off that mortgage that she has on the house over her head." Completely overcome, he turned away to hide the moisture gathering in his eyes.

It was not merely the contemplation of the pecuniary loss, great as it was, that so moved him, but the sudden demolition of hopes, the dearest and sweetest, which he had allowed to curl, twine and to take root in a heart that had few affections, and fewer weaknesses. How many times had his gaze wandered over the beautiful mare with scrutiny after she had been "called on" in her work. Not a muscle from stifle to fetlock escaped his hand, light and sensitive, to detect puff or strain, and unblemished, she remained sound as a dollar, with appetite unimpaired. It was human-nature to shut his eyes, and in fancy hear the roar of the ring rampant in victory. And to hear the multitudinous congratulations that would be showered upon him. Ah! how bitter was the awakening. How hard the sober reality, now to face. There seemed to nothing before him but the misery of defeat.

"Don't fret, Mr. Davis," said Mrs. Chetwyn kindly; "the darkest hour is before day."

The trainer shook his head, refusing comfort, but he watched the lady with some interest as she fearlessly approached the fractious steed after a concentrated gaze lasting not over thirty seconds, unheeding the warnings of the two men who were being dragged about like children, that she would have "her brains kicked out." Without hesitation she placed her pretty hand on the mare's arching frothy neck, gently cooing in her soft voice, "Soi, she place soi, you beauty." An instantaneous impression was made of the heart and mind of La Sylphide, and she lowered her head to be stroked, testifying unbounded approval of the new comer, who, taking the reins in her own hand, commanded the attendants to let her go. And pulling the off stirrup over, bounded into the saddle, and galloped away through the open gate and out upon the track.

Helpless, Mr. Chetwyn looked after her, his heart in his mouth.

Once, twice, thrice the frolicsome pair careened around the mile course. The lady then cantered back, and gleefully springing to the ground, exclaimed: "What a glorious creature she is! She moves like a bird! I am in love with her." Her affections were fully returned; La Sylphide had never been so happy in her life, and seemed ready to jump out of her skin with delight as she frisked around, and fawned upon Mrs. Chetwyn, who laughingly said: "Behave yourself, you dear foolish creature; I am going to put you right back into your stall. The mare submitted with admirable docility.

The lady then returned to her husband, whose appearance did not indicate approbation, and she promptly began: "Now don't scold, Jack. It was such a pleasure."

"A pleasure," he replied with asperity, "that I shall take special care you will not enjoy again. I never was so terribly frightened in my life."

"Well, don't beat me," she said, with a merry laugh. Her gaiety was so infectious that his brow cleared. "Now, Jackey," she continued in a mellifluent tone, "don't make an old woman of yourself, but go and have all-round look at the horses, while I attempt to comfort poor Mr. Davis. I believe he is weeping."

She carried the trainer off with her for a little distance. What she said to him nobody hear, but she talked long and earnestly. When she turned to come away no one could have said that Mr. Davis was weeping. But he looked like a man sentenced to death. Mrs. Chetwyn, on the contrary, seemed in the highest spirits, her face wearing a commingled look of exultation and resolve—such as probably glorified the face of Deceus when he made his heroic plunge, sacrificing life for his country; or as looked a noble martyr sublimely marching to the stake to meet a fiery death.

As Jack Chetwyn's wife came smilingly to meet him, he thought that she had never looked so bewilderingly lovely. Pardon him, reader, he is yet in the idiotic state incidental to initial matrimony, and he hoped that she was not going to ask to be allowed to ride La Sylphide again. He feared that it would not be possible to deny any request that she would make. She did not ask to ride La Sylphide, but she said, and her voice was low and sweet: "Jackey, my darlin, Aunt Rebecca is complaining a good deal and she wants me to pass a week or two with her. I do not like to refuse her, she was so kind to papa when he was all broken up after the war. It was her money that started him in business. But you will be busy with the horses and won't miss me."

"I will though, but I suppose Aunt Rebecca must have her way for this once."

"Of course she must. Now don't be a goose, jack. You can expect me to go with you to see La Sylphide win her race."

As they walked homeward, promenade a deux, her beguiling tongue brought him to a very hopeful view about the prospect of his horses: "They were all sound, and some hints had been given Mr. Davis, without wounding his feeling, about the management of La Sylphide."

Truth is might and will prevail, and it is useless to deny that Jack Chetwyn, left alone without the bright, buoyant presence which had so soon become to him what sunshine is to the flower, that his spirits sank rapidly. There is a popular superstition among horsemen to the effect that when racers by extraordinary good luck, which, in plain English, means good management, are brought up sound, and in blooming condition till the time is near at hand for them to face the starter, then, should one go amiss, a baneful epidemic is communicated, which will go through the stable. Also, that unfortunate IOU forged to the front insistently. "I don't know," he communed within himself, with commendable veracity, "what made me such a simpleton. I knew the dear little soul wasn't hungry for diamonds, but I had a yearning to give them to her. Well! Well! if the worst comes, I will sell the horses, and maybe some of the acres. Meanwhile I'll look sharp after the horses. And wouldn't it be a joy if La Sylphide should win."

Going to the stable he found old Mat in a horrible humor, apparently with cause, for the racers were taking their work well—only the mare was not visible.

"Why is not La Sylphide out?" asked Mr. Chetwyn.

Had old Mat been struck between the eyes, he could hardly have shown greater exasperation, but he answered: "I got her worked, somehow, this mornin' by herself, to keep her quiet." Scowling fiercely at the owner, he continued, "See here, Mr. Jack, I've got on my hands the biggest contract about that cussed mare that ever a man had; and if her race was well over, I'd almost be willin' to work for you the rest of my nateral life free, gratis, and for nothin'," he sighed deeply. "I've got to, not backin' out, to keep on with her. And I am goin' to do it my own way, and don't you interfere. I'm doin' all a man can do, and we've got a chance to win—if Providence don't split on us."

Mr. Chetwyn got "his message." To oppose a trainer is against all traditions, and the days passed bringing unmitigated discomfort to him, principally owing to the sustained ferocity of Mr. Davis' temper. What was being done with La Sylphide he did not dare to ask. For whole days he would sit on the topmost rail of the enclosure around the stable-buildings, gazing dumby at the mare's closely locked door. He missed his wife. He pined for the comfort she would be sure to give him. And how happy he felt on the day of her expected return—the eventful day of the mare's race. But in place of Mrs. Chetwyn, came a note, expressing regret, but saying it would not be possible for her to return him till late afternoon, and without her he must go to see La Sylphide win her race. Jack Chetwyn crushed the note in his hand, lost heart, and almost decided not to go to the races at all. A frightful picture rose before his eyes—La Sylphide brought on the track and acting like mad. In a despairing mood he walked to his stables, where there was a silence of death. He was briefly informed by Mr. Davis, who seemed the incarnation of rage, that only the mare would start today, and that she had been sent to the Association's track. "And now, Mr. Jack," snarled the trainer, "I've before me the hardest day's work mortal man ever had, and I won't be pestered with you. Jest you take you place in the grand stand, and stay there, no mater what happens, till our race is over. What's goin' to happen the Lord in heaven only knows. But I wish I was dead!"

The Kentucky Association is the oldest racing club in America—organized in 1826 by about fifty of the prominent turf men of central Kentucky. These gentlemen, passing away, were succeeded by others, who in turn made way for their successors. For long years this was the best racing in America, and characterized by decorum and fairness. Barring accidents, the best horses win. Each jockey knows that he must ride fair, and win if he can.

The world's best fighters had their moments of fear, and Jack Chetwyn had a strong inclination to "flicker"—to keep out of it, but with an effort he nerved himself to face the consequences. But he could not remember ever previously feeling so utterly miserable as when he passed through the entrance gate and made his way to the grand stand. Unsociable, he did not respond with cordiality to the many efforts made to engage him in conversation. "Excuse me," he said, hurrying on. "Well, stay long enough to tell us who it is with the outlandish name that is going to ride your mare."

"I really don't know. Somebody that Davis has picked up," answered Chetwyn, hurrying away. Looking after him a puzzled turfite said discontentedly: "I wonder what is the matter with Jack Chetwyn. He ought not to have got married if he's going to turn rusty on his old pals." A grave vice responded: "I have heard that his mare has been playing the dickens. That is a dispensation few can bear up under jovially—I have been there myself."

It was some minutes after, Mr. Chetwyn finding a seat, looked at the program held loosely in his hand. Thoughts of La Sylphide filled his brain; he began to hate the mare and to wish that she had died in infancy. Then he was conscious of a feeling of compassion for the unlucky chap going to ride her, and mechanically he sought out the name; and it was plain to read: "John Chetwyn's bay mare, La Sylphide, by Fellowcraft—dam Sylph by Imp. Glencoe; jockey Pheohki."

Jack Chetwyn was a high-minded, high bred American, and if he did not aspire to be dashingly courageous, he could always be decently collected, but he felt strangely unnerved at the sight of that name. Instinctively, it seemed a sinister warning—it affected him in a harassing way, as if someone he dearly loved were in peril. But the thought that his wife was safe with Aunt Rebecca, and he would soon have her to himself again, enabled him to shake off the depressing influence—measurably.

Second only to the inviolability of the Masonic secrets, were the affairs of a training stable. But let a horse go wrong, the birds of the air—the breezes of heaven seem to divulge it, and La Sylphide's misconduct had leaked out, and deeply anxious were those who had made investments in her. But of late the earth might as well have opened and swallowed her up, so little enlightenment had been obtained. It was now known, however, that in the early morning she had been brought to her quarters on the racing grounds. But no one had seen her. Not even for the preliminary gallop had she been brought out. And, not desiring a broken head, no one had asked questions of Mr. Davis who, looking like vengeance, sat in a splint-bottomed chair, tilted against the mare's door. When the order came to bring the mare on the track, his only reply was a brief mention of the place of torment. But when his own split-second timer informed him categorically that he had not an instant to lose, with a deep groan he arose, unlocked the door, and brought out the mare, giving her to the charge of one of the men. Then he brought out a lad completely wrapped in a a large coarse cloak. Little of him could be seen. From his blue cap his black hair descends in whisks, almost concealing his face. At the scales the cloak was removed, but a blue scarf swaddled his neck and face, the boy coughing and choking as if he would burst a blood-vessel.

He's got a cold," explained Mr. Davis gruffly, "and there wasn't no time left to change riders;" adding sardonically, "these jocks 'round here ain't none of them too keen to pilot this mare."

When lifted to the saddle the boy dropped into an ungainly lump. While the racers were lining up for the start, ol Mat, with firm hold of the bridle, said: "This mare is vicious. I wish I may die if she did not almost clean out that Favordale colt at Forham. I'll take her back'ards, and let her loose when the field is off—to prevent accidents."

When the start is made, horses off, the jockey on La Sylphide, still in a lump, made no effort to decrease the wide gap opened. The mare's backers were excited and wrathful, and a perfect storm burst from a frantic mob.

"Go along, boy! What are you hanging back for? Are you going to sleep?" some of the desperate ones would willingly revive the obsolete argumentum ad lipides.

"Bump on a log! He's going to mile!" roared a jubilant plunger whose money was not on La Sylphide.

The mare and jockey, seemingly of one mind about the pace—a "bad last" having no terror—take the "heart-breaking hill," where so many good horses have given up the ghost, so to speak, in exhaustion. But the hill was surmounted and then comes a surprise—the vast multitude almost ceased to breathe. The boy on La Sylphide uplifts himself, and sat down to ride. The willing mare, given her head, and rapidly passing a tiring field, shoots to the front, and comes flying down the stretch with a flight of speed never witnessed before by the oldest race-goers, and reaches the winning post an easy winner.

People look at one another in amazement when the time for the mile and quarter is hung out: 2:7 ½ the fastest time ever made on the Lexington track—and not since equaled.

After the weighing in, old Mat, like a whirlwind, pounced upon the boy, and throwing the cloak around him and carrying him in his arms, thrusting him into a waiting carriage, shouts to the coachman: "Drive like lightning."

A wondrous joy lights up his homely face as he receives into his own hands the bridle-reins of the gallant mare.

Winning a race in marvelous time does not constitute the best and purest joy, but it is very dazzling and seductive.

Old Mat's dream of victory is realized with its corollary of felicities. His name is shouted, and congratulations galore. Many rush eagerly to touch his hand. Others, that cannot get near enough, reach over and touch him with their walking sticks.

Catching sight of Mr. Chetwyn, he shouted: "We win, Mr. Jack."[2]

b. Sue Munday

Frank Logan (New York, 1904)
"Rebellion long in his way, and he found it."

Eastern Kentucky had been cleared of guerillas, though in the central part of the state small bands showed themselves from time to time apparently with no other object than to seize United States mails, for what purpose was not clear, as the unrifled mail-bags were usually discovered without much loss of time thrown into some ditch.

But the time came when a large extent of the country was amazed and shocked by the outrages perpetrated by a band of "Irregular Troops," as they called themselves, and claiming allegiance to the Southern Confederacy, and strangest of all under the leadership of a young woman, to obtain, as it was said, revenge for a murdered sweetheart.

Many efforts had been made for her capture, but all in vain. The men under her lead fought like demons, often driving back—pell-mell—bodies of troops ten times larger than their own. They seemed actually to defy danger. Only in large towns were the Federal troops secure from their attacks.

Mounted on "pressed" race-horses they scoured the country. To dash up and fire into a Federal camp was almost a daily occurrence.

At other times they would fiercely assail a Federal column on the march, cheered on by a clear young voice shouting, "Ride over them, men! Shoot! Kill!" And disappear almost as suddenly as they had appeared, leaving traces of their handiwork in many an empty saddle, scattering among the hills safe from pursuit.

There is nothing so demoralizing as fear, and among soldiers no sentiment is so dangerously contagious. At times they have been known to fall into that state where "a thousand might well be stopped by three."

At camp fires Sue Munday and her exploits were the sole topics of interest. Their fear of her had deepened and strengthened into superstition; many declared that they had seen her shot clean through the body and no harm had come of it. "Yes," cried an excited voice, "I once got a thundering good jab at her myself with my bayonet, and I expected to see her drop off her horse, but by all the devils! If she didn't turn square around, and whack me over the head senseless, with her smoking revolver, with the ugliest cussing I ever heard in all my life. It's not my belief the ammunition issued out to us by Government will ever fetch her. And if I had as much as a silver quarter—greenback fractional currency won't do—I'd mold it into a bullet for her. I would, by hokey!"

"You are right," acquiesced many voices; "lead and steel won't hurt the likes of her."

This existing feeling the commanding general found to be extremely inconvenient; the soldiers were confessedly reluctant to go out on scouting duty, and in truth were disinclined for any duty—from time immemorial soldiers have been so affected when convinced, "luck is agin us"—and recently in his own proper person the General had suffered an indignity. A baggage train had been stopped by the redoubtable Sue, and a suit of his own uniform captured. The train was burned, and the escort—all not killed in the fight—after being sworn in to support the Southern Confederacy, were detailed, under the mockery of a flag of truce, for the service of returning to the owner the suit of clothes saved from the burning, with the request to "send in exchange some articles suitable for woman's wear for the Captain's use."

A person laughed at is a person insulted, with all the rights of the situation, and the General's ire was so roused that he expressed his determination to catch the "limb of Satan," if it took every man in the State of Kentucky to do it.

Mighty preparations were being made. A mounted brigade, with three days' cooked rations, ordered for the expedition.

On the day before the contemplated move the commanding general was favored with a call at his headquarter from Colonel Logan. This officer rarely made visits of ceremony; more often, his visits were of a nature distinctly disagreeable. On various occasions he "peculiar ideas" on the conduct of the war had been announced with unvarnished bluntness.

Burning the houses of non-combatants because of "Southern sympathies," and destroying, or appropriating their other property, did not seem to him the best way to inculcate in their hearts a love and veneration for the Union.

Nor did he think the hanging and shooting of men merely because they had relations in the Rebel army, the most approved way of fostering their allegiance to the National Government. But his "peculiar ideas" had not made many converts among his brother officers, and he was too valuable an officer to be dispensed with, and it being well known he would stand neither threats nor reproofs, he was valued accordingly. And on this occasion his pomp of word was singularly unostentatious. He curtly asked for a week's leave of absence, without any of the glittering generalities relating to "urgent private business," or the more pressing urgency of "indisposition"—though it would be impossible to associate the latter cause with the appearance and bearing of the stalwart cavalryman.

The General looking at him gravely said:

"May I ask you, Colonel Logan, why, at this time, you prefer such a request?"

"You may," was the answer. "And while I will fight men against any odds—no one has yet accused me of not being able to ride middling straight—and when my own men have been dismounted for any particular service, to keep them from whimpering, I have left my horse and footed it with them, and have always been ready to take the lead with an ax or a spade, but I'm damned if I go on this woman hunt. I refuse obedience, and it is not worth your while to give me any orders. You can have my sword if you like."

The chief reflected for a moment. He had a unlimited capacity for saying No, and for being fractious when crossed, but on this occasion he decided to temporize replying:

"I will, of course, Colonel Logan, grant you the furlough you wish, but you had better reconsider, and go with us on this expedition. You have great influence over the men. This woman has, as you know, been playing the wild with such audacity and impunity that the devil appears to have had her in charge—he can help his votaries at a pinch—but there are limits to his powers, and if by the providence of God she should fall into our hands, in their state of exasperation, I might need you help to prevent the men from roasting her alive."

"There is some truth in that," was the answer. "The men have all been in such a scare they might be devilish if she were caught. But there is a large-sized if in the way. My own opinion is, the first glimpse of her blue cap will skedaddle the men, but even so, there will be left you and I and perhaps some of the officers to give battle to Captain Sue and the sixty men at her back. Though I do not believe she will stay to be found, but will maneuver to keep us dodging after her among the hills till men and horses are tired out, and we will have to sneak back into Louisville without having seen hide or hair of any of the gang—unless they are betrayed. That may happen. And while I will go with you, I repeat, it is business I preeminently don't hanker after." Giving the salute, he withdrew.

The General gave a curiously complacent smile. "In dealing with my recalcitrant Colonel," quoth he, "I was forced to whittle my authority down to rather a fine point. But unless I am much mistaken, my fastidious gentleman, when once afield, will join in the worry with zest, and it wouldn't surprise me any if he is the very man to lay hands on the lovely Sue—stranger things have happened. The 'roasting' was a flight of my imagination, but if I am lucky enough to catch her, hang she will."

Very imposing was the appearance of the Federal brigade as it filed out of Louisville in columns of fours. The showy uniforms, rattling scabbards, jingling spurs, flying banners, are looked upon by a large per centum of the citizens without neutrality of feeling—every spectator was either fish or flesh. Some cheered heartily and loudly. Others gave a silent but ultra-fervent benediction—of the wrong sort.

Scouts in countrymen's dress had already been sent out to locate Captain Munday.

Colonel Logan riding by the General's side laughed sarcastically, and said:

"Is not this something very like an elephant after a little mouse?"

"Perhaps so," was the acquiescent answer, "and I know of no reason why the sharp and continual bites of a little mouse may not at last goad an elephant into revolt—we have never heard that the great Caesar did not wince at mosquito bites. But Miss Munday, or Captain Munday, cannot be likened to either a mouse or a mosquito—she has the efficiency of a *corps d'armee*, and if her work is not very soon stopped I must look to be superseded."

On the alert, and in close columns they pushed ahead leisurely, not to unwind the horses, rendering them incapable of giving chase.

About two o'clock on the afternoon of the next day runners came in, and reported the "Munday gang" not two miles distant, and ready for some enterprise—certainly not flight—as they were mounted, and heavily armed, and waiting, evidently aware of the approaching foe.

Turning to Colonel Logan, the General said, "It looks as if she intends trying her old trick —dashing up, firing rapidly, and showing clean heels. But, perhaps, this time, Miss Munday may find herself surprised and disappointed—that card won't win this game."

His orders were given deliberately, and executed with celerity, and in silence. Gradually around that little band the Union troops were massed with the utmost caution, keeping well within supporting distance, until their arrondissement was complete. Then the blue ranks moved nearer and nearer, closer and closer, until a halt was called, something like the grace sometimes shown by a vindictive cat to a little mouse within her easy reach.

From his point of view Frank Logan could see that small band with great distinctness. And at once he singled out the central figure around which the others seemed grouped as mere accessories.

There is no denying that a graceful figure is of the first attraction and leads to the inspection of faultless face. And there is no gainsaying that it is a necessity of man's nature to delight in the contemplation of beauty, though there may be no personal interest—it is only cause and effect, and Frank Logan was instantly seized with a strong emotion of pity, with a great desire to save her.

Mounted on a superb horse of extraordinary beauty of the rich color and commanding size of the Yorkshire blood, Sue Monday looked a Bellona. She wore a blue skirt Zouave jacket, silk plush cap, from which her jetty curls had escaped, and caught by the light breeze streamed out in careless abundance. Erect in her stirrups she stood surveying her foes, showing not a trace of womanly fear or indecision. With the swiftness of light she seemed to comprehend the situation and to form her orders in a low voice, not reaching the enemy:

"Fall into ranks, men! Not too deep! Keep your alignments close and strong—all depends on that. Now take your bridles in your teeth, draw your pepper boxes, and ride slap through and over them—wait for the work, then shoot fast, but don't lose a load. Forward!"

Putting their chargers in motion, they came with the fury of a cyclone.

Frank Logan felt himself as one placed in a dreadful strait, but the soldier-instinct was true, his voice rose loud and sonorous—he still wishes to save her—"Attention. Steady, men! Prepare to receive cavalry. Corral them with your sabers."

In one moment the glittering blades flash in the sunlight, and stationary, seem to present an impassable barrier. But undismayed, on they come. Sue Munday's band, with the furious dash of the highborn, high-mettled horses they ride, not firing a shot until within ten paces, then, as if a blot had struck from heaven, a sheet of fire leaps out and runs along in front of the advancing line. Again, and again, and again, continuously flashes that awful flame, men and horses going down under it in indiscriminate heaps.

On they come, the noble horses springing over the dead and dying. All would have escaped had there not been one accidental shot wounding Munday's lieutenant at her side.

"Drop your pistols, McGruder, and cling to your pommel," she shouted, catching her wounded comrade's bridle. It was a fatal move for her; the instant lost gave Frank Logan the opportunity to press over and clasp her in his arms. With a groan, the wounded McGruder dropped from his horse, in the agonies of death. See this, Sue Munday gave a cry of unspeakable wrath. In seizing McGruder's bridle she had lost her pistols, and held as in a vise, she could use neither Winchester nor saber. Helpless, without means of defense, yet she looked fierce defiance into the face so close to her own, and opening her beautiful red lips, poured forth a torrent, a deluge of profanity.

Frank Logan looked at her intently for a moment or two, then dropping her to the ground, shook her roughly.

The General, who was not far off, witnessed this amazing scene.

"Gracious!" he exclaimed to an officer at this side, "what has come over Logan? Look at him! He was down on the 'woman hunt' before we left Louisville, but evidently he has got into the spirit of it, and joins in the worry as savagely as the youngest hound of the pack." Galloping up, he said with mock moderation, "Stop abusing the female, Logan."

Frank Logan turned square around, his face fiery red with excitement and anger—and his words were not Addisonian—"Female h___! I don't pretend to the advantages of a college education, but I know a man from a woman. Here, a couple of you men; just take that jacket and petticoat from this lovely chap."

The grinning soldiers; nothing loth, obeyed, and soon a very handsome young man, very angry, clad in shirt and trousers, stood revealed. Once again Colonel Logan took up his parable: "Here, General, I have the honor to present to you Miss Munday, at your service. The same young lady who has been scaring us all nearly to death."

This was a reminder. The mirth of the soldiers quickly gave place to rage.

They had been so honestly and supernaturally afraid of "Sue Munday," who was in reality only a mere boy. They were proceeding to handle him roughly.

"Stop that, you curs," commanded Colonel Logan. "Are you trying to take it out of him for having shown him your backs so often? Some of you bring the fellow's horse. I'll take charge of the late Miss Munday myself."

After a burst of what Frank Logan thought to be the most vehement and the wickedest swearing he had ever heard in his life, the young fellow was haughtily silent—disdaining complaints.

Riding by his side, Colonel Logan looked at him compassionately, confessing in his own heart that Munday was a gallant youth who might have escaped with the others but for his generous effort to carry off a wounded comrade. In kindly tones, he said, "I will protect you from ill-treatment until we reach Louisville; there my power will end, and I fear you must prepare for the worst. What could have induced you to take to such a life?"

"Take to such a life!" was the quick rejoinder. "This was the way of it, when you kill us it is nothing. But if we kill you it is murder, no matter what the provocation. My home was burned, my two elder brothers shot. And those who were with me—I am glad of their escape; they will at you again—were forced to leave their homes with no other prospects in view than fighting by day, marching by night, and to be ill-fed, ill sheltered, with no amelioration of their hardships but the love of the soil they were trying to defend, and the thought it was their country whose wrongs we have tried to avenge. Well, for a long time we rode right merrily, and played our part right well, though we knew it was not the life best calculated for the making of old bones, and I am resigned to be a victim. A sacrifice I may say; and having faced death a thousand times, I can meet it as a brave man should."

Nothing more was said between the two, and almost immediately after reaching Louisville, Marcellus Jerome Clark was executed.[3]

c. Selected Poetry, *Lexington Herald* (1902–1905)

Autumn (October 1902)

Autumn comes, we see in the eve's shortening hours,
In the yellowed tint of mid-summer's flowers,
In the wild wind's moan as it winds o'er the lea,
In the rustling of leaves as they fall from the tree.
All things tell of moments flying,
Bloom of earth sheen less and dying.
The corn for the reaper is ready and waiting.
Fruits of the orchards ripe for the taking.
Those who have planted and tilled the soil
A harvest will find to reward their toil.
And the fear of a lack will never lurk,
To trouble the night when no man can work.
But those who in season neglected to sow,
And past idly time for labor below,
When they look for a crop in fields of their care,
They will find only weeds and rubbish are there.
Too late now to plant, the seedtime is o'er;
Hours fled will return no more.
Oh! May we all plant, and work while we may,
To replenish and garner for the endless day,
For the soul which has provided no store
Will want when the harvest forever is o'er.
Life on this earth only is given
To prepare for the eternal banquet of Heaven.

Ode to Winter (January 1904)

Hail to winter's tempestuous breeze!
The shouts of its might fall on the ear
As it bends and breaks the forest trees,
Crushing, snapping, the beautiful here.

Sunshine is not for storms in the breast,
Coming of memory of vanished years,
Soft winds belong to that era most blest,
When springtime harbored not tears.

In high chanson it wails o'er sleeping dead,
Those who were loved in years that are gone,
They heed not, they hear not, their spirits are fled,
To a haven of peace, safe from a storm.
Oh! raise your loved clamor and revel in strife,
And tumultuously sweep through the air,
For your reign will, like the winter of life,
Yield to a spring radiantly fair.

El Dolorosa (June 1904)

List! to the Song of the cooing dove,
The sad-sweetness breathed in his lay;
Does it tell of a deep, disquieting love
Afflicting his heart—his mate away?
The mate returned—he sings of woe,
His mournful voice rising o'er the lea,
Still unchecked comes sorrow's flow
Her presence does not, cannot, free.

Why ever grieving, sorrowful dove?
Will your lament never, never, be still?
Your olive-branch is a token of love,
The promise of peace and good will.

Why doomed ever-lacking the nest
Outward borne with tireless wing?
What hast done to plant in your breast
A cureless wound forever to sting?

Dos't mourn when from the ark sent
To see if God's people could return to earth?
You went not back tho the flood was spent
And the purified world fair as at birth.

Oh, tis ever thus! A trust betrayed
Its sure, avenging mark will set,
And the faithless hear, dismayed
Is burdened with a long regret.

The Equal Grave (March 1905)
(De Soto and Pilot Bledsoe)

"The Father of Waters!" De Soto rapturously cried,
When the broad, rolling river he first descried.
Would his rapture been less, his heart less brave,
Had he known how soon he would be "neath its wave
Visions of empire gone—his bright eyes closed—
And hands folded meekly in eternal repose.
To keep his death secret from savage ears
His stricken comrades with flooding tears
Hid in a rude, oak trough his body from sight,
And in the gloom of a tempestuous night,
Silently, when the night and morning meet,
Delivered it to the care of that mighty deep.
Sleep well, great Captain in your honored rest,
And legends of glory will never depart
From the valiant soldier with tender heart.

Three centuries later, human life to save,
Another hero found the equal grave

****

Over the Mississippi's wide expanse,
The bright sun's rays gleam and dance,
As a steamer plies its way of leisure
Filled with those who thought of pleasure;
The merry laugh comes quick and clear,
And the babbling gay, so sweet to hear,
None to dream, or whisper with bated breath
The solemn warning, "In life we are in death."
T'was joy, only joy that reigned supreme,
And life fair as an enchanted dream,
One moment more, the change how dire!
The shouting rose: The boat's on fire!
The Captain's voice is heard above the din
As he rushed the upper deck to win.
Pilot, the boat's on fire! Head for land!
Keep to your wheel while able to stand!
The answer is slangy—the words only few,
But they ring out spontaneous and true:
I'll get her there! And I'll do more!
I'll hold her there till the peops are all on shore!
True to his word, the wheel flew round
Nearing to safety with each rebound.
But with cruel haste the moments fly,
And freighted with such deep agony.
The red flames rise up—higher! higher!
Look, heaven, look! The wheel's on fire!
Steadfast stands that heroic man—alone.
Have pity, God!—his hands are gone!
Faithful still to avert appalling harms,
He clasps his wheel with mutilated arms.
The flames surround—he is seen no more,
But his work is done; the peops on shore
And in that raging, awful, funeral pyre
Bledsoe willed to anguish, and expire,
With courage sublime, he met the extreme test,
And what is so grand as a man at his best;
Flow on great river with magnificent wave,
Down in your depths is a martyr's grave.
Blow gently soft winds o'er the hallow'd spot,
Bringing incense from the forget-me-not,
And a requiem sing, oh! birds of air,
For that glorious man buried there.

d. Notes from the 1899 "Annual Catalogue of Brood Mares"

Ashland Thoroughbred Stock Farm, Founded by Henry Clay, 1830

Mrs. John M. Clay, Proprietor
Lexington, Kentucky

The breeding of Thoroughbred horses at Ashland had its beginning as a pastime for its owner, H. Clay, anterior to 1831. Susan, by the Darnaby Diomed, was the first matron. A stud book was duly opened, and on its second left-hand page, in his own handwriting is given the pedigree and description of Susan. On the opposite page he states: "she has a bay filly with the following marks:"—(a space was left for the marks, but they were never set down) . . . His entries continued, giving a faithful record of what his mares had done, together with their sins of omission. Occasionally descriptions of the foals were given with a verbosity that borders on ostentation; but generally he left a space for the marks, which remained unfilled.

His last entry said: "Another bay mare, by Kocklani, had a bay colt by Monarch, the 5th of May, 1842, with he following marks:"—but the marks were not given. His son John then took the Thoroughbred stock in charge. Important additions had been made to the brood mares; but the most valuable of all Magnolia and Margaret Wood came later, and under his able management their produce came immediately to the fore front, and performed with distinguished merit on almost every race course in America. He bred Maggie B. B., dam of Iroquois the Derby winner at Epson, 1881. She was sold by him as a two-year-old under the name of Magpie.

He also bred Sachem, who ran third in the same classic event for the year 1882. It was his invariable custom to keep only a limited number of strictly first-class mares, and he bred so many good winners that he was called "the Sir Joseph Hawley of America." It was his unchangeable opinion that broken-down race mares—no matter of what renown on the turf—were not the best specimens for the production of high class racers, and the females selected by him to retain for brood mares were never excessively raced, and more often never trained at all. La Sylphide was immediately withdrawn from the turf after lowering the mile-and-a-quarter record. And his long career of almost unbroken success proved the correctness of his views.

The management has now fallen into not very competent hands; but the honest effort which sometimes supplies the place of ability will be used to keep the stock, at least approximately, at the standard of excellence hitherto maintained.

Notes

Preface and Acknowledgements

1. Following is a list of the signatures from the top left corner (clockwise): Maj. Gen. Edmund Pendleton Gaines, commander of the militias in the Seminole Indian War; J. M. Botts, Representative from Virginia, Henry Clay's mess mate in 1840; Daniel Webster, Senator from Boston and rival of Henry Clay; Carolyn LeRoy Webster (Mrs. Daniel Webster); William C. Geston, Representative from North Carolina, supporter of John Quincy Adams; Nathaniel Parker Willis, author and editor who visited Ashland, the estate of Henry Clay, in 1852; Dolly Payne Madison, First Lady and Washington hostess; Carolyn LeRoy Webster; Winfield Scott, General in Mexican American War; Willie Person Mangum, Representative from North Carolina; John Quincy Adams, sixth U. S. President; John E. Wood, Kentucky newspaper editor; Robert C. Winthrop, Representative and Senator from Boston, author of a memoir of Henry Clay; Daniel Webster.

2. William H. Townsend, *Lincoln and the Bluegrass: Slavery and Civil War in Kentucky* (Lexington, 1955), 291–292.

3. Nicholas Breton, "Truth" (1616), copied in the handwriting of Dolly P. Madison on August 23, 1847, Washington, D. C. Breton was an English author of religious poems.

4. Wallace Stegner, *Angle of Repose* (New York, 1971), 24.

5. Lyman H. Weeks, ed., *An Historical Account of Racing in the United States* (New York, 1998), 168.

6. Ojos Morenos [pseudonym], *What Will the World Say?: A Novel of Every-Day Life; and Only a Woman* (Philadelphia, 1873). Mrs. John M. Clay, *Some Little of the Angel Still Left: A Novel* (Cincinnati, 1893). Mrs. John M. Clay, *Uncle Phil: A Novel* (New York, 1899), Second Edition (New York, 1901). Mrs. John M. Clay, *Frank Logan: A Novel* (New York, 1901). Mrs. John M. Clay, *The Sport of Kings: Racing Stories* (New York, 1912).

Prologue

1. Charles Staples, *The History of Pioneer Lexington* (Lexington, 1939), 158, 215.

2. Robert V. Remini, *Henry Clay, Statesman for the Union* (New York, 1991), 18–19.

3. Louis des Cognets, *The Russell Family of Virginia* (Lexington, 1960). The book also includes an earlier 1884 family history *William Russell and His Descendants* by Anna R. des Cognets. A different and critical view of the early history of the Russell family can be found in "Lt. Col. William Russell (ca. 1699–1757), A Critical Examination" by George Ely Russell, *The Virginia Genealogist,* 1978.

4. Robert Seager II, ed., *The Papers of Henry Clay,* Vol. 8 (Lexington, 1984), 310.

5. Remini, *Henry Clay*, 373.

6. *History of Callaway County Missouri* (1884). Reprinted by the Kingdom of Callaway County Historical Society (Independence, Missouri, 2001), 269–272.

7. Robert A Caro, *Master of the Senate: The Years of Lyndon Johnson* (New York, 2002), 17–18.

Part I. Josephine Russell Travels with Her Father

Chapter 1.

1. Mrs. John M. Clay, "Autumn," *Lexington Herald*, October, 1902. See Appendix c.

2. Louis des Cognets, *The Russell Family in Virginia* (Lexington, 1960), 70–83. According to the "Kentucky Historic Resources Inventory" (1980), Lexington-Fayette County Historic Commission, the original stone house named Poplar Hill was built in 1791. A larger house on the property designed by Robert M. McMeekin was built in 1928, and the old stone house was then used as a tenant or guest house. For background about the Russell homes, see Elizabeth M. Simpson, *Bluegrass Houses and Their Traditions* (Lexington, 1932), 131–140 and 367–374 and Mrs. John M. Clay, "Two Old Russell Homes on the Russell Road," *Lexington Herald*, November 28, 1915.

3. Ibid., 73.

4. Mrs. John M. Clay, "Two Old Russell Homes on the Russell Road."

5. Mrs. John M. Clay, *Uncle Phil* (New York, 1901), 18.

6. Louis des Cognets, *The Russell Family of Virginia*, 70–84 and 276–277. Thomas Allen Russell remained in central Kentucky where he purchased Ash Hill on the Russell Cave Road. He became a member of the Kentucky Legislature and High Sheriff of Fayette County. He was the eighth member of the Russell family to hold that office.

7. In the 1840's the Russell family letters were from Bluffton. According to the Callaway County Historical Society, this was a small community at that time on the banks of the Missouri River.

8. Zaenett Russell to Mrs. Priscilla G. Freeland, December 11, 1836.

9. Callaway County Historical Society website (http://history.fulton.missouri.org/)

10. William LaBach, "The Ancestry of William H. Russell" (http://members.tripod.com/~labach/whrussan.htm); Special Census of California, 1852, Monterey Public Library. The children born to the family of William H. Russell and Zaenett Russell were:

- Robert Eugene Russell born in Kentucky ca. 1825.
- Egbert Freeland Russell born in Kentucky ca. 1827.
- Frederick William Russell born in Kentucky ca. 1830.
- Thomas Allen Russell born in Kentucky ca. 1832.
- Josephine Deborah Russell born in Callaway County, Missouri, 1835.
- Henry Clay Russell born in Callaway County, Missouri, 1836.
- George Washington Russell born in Callaway County, Missouri, 1838.

11. Mrs. John M. Clay, *Uncle Phil* (New York, 1901),17.

12. Ibid., 40.

13. Louisiana Wood Simpson, "The Colonel's Lady, The Life and Loves of Josephine Russell, An American Heroine and Daughter-In-Law of Henry Clay" (Lexington, 1981), 2–3. This booklet, prepared for children that visit Ashland, the estate of Henry Clay, includes several stories about Josephine's travels as a young girl.

14. Mrs. John M. Clay, *Uncle Phil* (1901).

15. *History of Callaway County Missouri (Independence, 2001)*, 269–272.

16. U. S. Census in Missouri 1840; the Callaway County Historical Society; William H. Russell to Thomas Russell, ca. 1843.

17. Seager, ed., *The Papers of Henry Clay*, Vol. 9, Henry Clay to William H. Russell, July 27, 1842, 747.

18. Daniel Webster to William H. Russell, July 26, 1841.

19. William H. Russell, "A Federal Circuit and District Court in Missouri," December 22, 1841.

20. Nathaniel P. Willis, *Health Trip to the Tropics* (New York, 1852). This book contains a detailed description of a visit to Ashland.

21. Seager, ed., *The Papers of Henry Clay*, Vol. 9, Henry Clay to Albert G. Boone, July 11, 1843, 834.

22. Ibid., Henry Clay to William H. Russell, May 11, 1843, 818.

23. Mrs. John M. Clay, "Henry Clay: By Mrs. John M. Clay," *Lexington Leader*, April 6, 1902.

24. Note written by Henry Clay, July 1843. UK

25. Mrs. John M. Clay, *Sport of Kings*, 8.

26. Remini, *Henry Clay*, 29–31.

27. Lucretia Erwin Simpson, "Ashland Thoroughbred Stock Farm," ca. 1920. Unpublished. Copy is on file at Ashland, the estate of Henry Clay.

28. For the history of the early Thoroughbred farms, see Kent Hollingsworth, *The Kentucky Thoroughbred* (Lexington, 1985). Mrs. John M. Clay's description of the early days of Ashland Stock Farm can be found in Appendix d.

29. James Barbour to Henry Clay, July 22, 1835. UK Describes *Allegrante*'s pedigree and proposes going halves on *Allegrante* and other horses for $500. A letter from Henry Clay to James Barbour confirmed his purchase of the horses for $1,000.

30. Ibid.

31. Zanette is one of several variations in the spelling of Mrs. William H. Russell's first name used by family and friends. Mrs. Zaenett Russell is the name on her tombstone in the Lexington Cemetery.

32. Thomas A. Russell to William H. Russell, December 17, 1843. This letter also contains a description of the famous fight between Cassius M. Clay and Samuel Brown at a political rally in August, 1843 at the old Russell home on the Russell Cave Pike. Thomas A. Russell served as High Sheriff of Fayette County.

33. Mrs. John M. Clay, "Henry Clay," *Lexington Herald*, April 6, 1902.

Chapter 2.

1. Mrs. John M. Clay, "El Dolorosa," *Lexington Herald,* June, 1904. See Appendix c.

2. Statement of William Breadwell to the Fulton County Court, March 23, 1846.

3. Edwin Bryant, *What I Saw in California By Wagon from Missouri to California in 1847–1848.* Reprinted by The Narrative Press (Santa Barbara, CA., 2001).

4. Bernard DeVoto, *The Year of Decision: 1846* (New York, 1942), 148.

5. *History of Callaway County Missouri*, 269–272.

6. Website describing old Fort Bridger (http://www.isu.edu/~trinmich/FtBridger.html).

7. William H. Russell to Thomas A. Russell, July 1846.

8. Ibid., 183–186.

9. DeVoto, *The Year of Decision: 1846*, tells the story of the Donner Party and other events during this period.

10. Zaenett Russell to Col. Thomas A Russell, June 8, 1846.

11. Charles Kerr, ed., *History of Kentucky,* Vol. IV (Chicago and New York, 1922), 314–315, and the papers of Mrs. Minor E. Simpson.

12. Clay Street in San Francisco was named for Henry Clay at a later date.

13. H. H. Bancroft, *History of California,* Vol. 5, Pioneer Register and Index, 316.

14. For a daily narrative of the formation of the California Battalion and the defeat of the Mexicans, see the final chapters of *What I Saw in California* by Edwin Bryant.

15. The red and yellow striped scarf has an attached note about the incident.

16. Bryant, 275 and William H. Russell to Thomas A. Russell, Los Angeles 1847.

17. Bryant, 389–390.

18. Bryant, 391–392 and DeVoto, 471–472.

19. Melba Porter Hay, ed., *The Papers of Henry Clay,* Vol. 10 (Lexington, 1991), 332, Henry Clay to Zaenett Russell, June 2, 1847.

20. William Y. Chalfant, *Dangerous Passage, The Sante Fe Trail and the Mexican War* (Norman, OK, 1994), 73–86.

21. DeVoto, 479–481.

22. Jacob's sister, Susan, married Henry Clay's son James.

23. Ibid.

24. Melba Porter Hay, ed., *The Papers of Henry Clay,* Vol. 10, 823–824. Henry Clay to Alexander H. H. Stuart, October 22, 1850.

25. Mary Ellen Ryan and Gary S. Breschini, "Influence of the Gold Rush," Monterey County Historical Society, (http://users.dedot.com/mchs/goldrush.html).

26. Pearl Wilcox, *Jackson County Pioneers* (Independence, MO, 1975), 232.

27. Ibid.

28. Simpson, "The Colonel's Lady," 2–3.

29. "William Henry Russell," *Dictionary of American Biography* (New York, 1995). Russell's law partner, Edward D. Baker became U. S. Senator from Oregon and was the only member of Congress killed in the Civil War, (http://www.senate.gov/artandhistory/history/minute/Senator_Killed_In_Battle.htm).

30. 1850 U. S. Federal Census, California, Monterey County.

31. Ryan and Breschini, "Influence of the Gold Rush." Monterey County Historical Society (http://users.dedot.com/mchs/goldrush.html).

32. Letter Fragment in the handwriting of Josephine Russell, ca. 1850.

33. 1850 U. S. Federal Census, Town of Monterey, Ca. Public Library of Monterey.

34. Ted Morgan, *A Shovel of Stars* (New York, 1995), 173.

35. Melba Porter Hay, ed., *The Papers of Henry Clay*, Vol. 10, 823–824. Henry Clay to Alexander H. H. Stuart, October 22, 1850.

36. Ibid., 876–877. Henry Clay to Millard Fillmore, early March, 1851.

37. Mrs. John M. Clay, *Uncle Phil*, 18.

38. Susan J. Hargous refers to him in correspondence about Josephine's return trip.

39. Robert W. Foster to Josephine Russell, May 11, 1851. UK

40. Asa Bement Clarke, *Travels in Mexico and California* (1852: reprinted College Station, TX, 1988), 43.

41. Mrs. John M. Clay, *The Sport of Kings*, 61.

42. Carl Sartorius, *Mexico about 1850* (Stuttgart, 1961), 2–49.

43. The papers of Josphine Clay's daughter, Mrs. Minor E. Simpson.

Chapter 3.

1. Susan J. Hargous to Josephine Russell, August 13, 1851.

2. *History of Callaway County Missouri*, 269–272. A search of the microfilm records of the *Daily Alta Californian* by the historian at Monterey Public Library did not find the article.

3. Mrs. John M. Clay, "The Equal Grave," *Lexington Herald*, March, 1906. See Appendix c.

4. U. S. Census of Population, Monterey County, California 1850. Monterey Public Library.

5. German Information Center (New York, 1976), (http://uweb.superlink.net/czorn/library/JohannSutter.html.)

6. Family story; Simpson, "The Colonel's Lady," 4.

7. "Operations of Sailor Thieves," *Daily Alta Californian*, January 8, 1853 (www.meritimeheritage.org/captains/bio).

8. Ibid.

9. Donald Thomas Clark, *Monterey County Place Names: A Geographical Dictionary* (Carmel Valley, CA: Kestrel Press, 1991), 406. Refers to Mussel Point (now called Cabrillo Point) on the Monterey Pensinsula. Mussels could be harvested along the coast until recent times.

10. Mrs. John M. Clay, *Uncle Phil* (New York, Rev. Ed. 1901), 24–36.

11. Douglas Ottinger to Josephine Russell, March 27, 1851.

12. Maria to Josephine Russell, April 12 (ca. 1852).

13. Ibid., November 13, 1852.

14. Captain Douglas Ottinger established the first "Life Saving Stations" of the U. S. Coast Guard, and was created with the discovery of Humboldt Bay, California. In 1865, he commanded the first revenue steamer *Perry* with many successful rescues at sea. See "Coast Guard Pioneer," *The U. S. Coast Guard*, November, 1931, 12.

15. Kent Masterson Brown, "The Colonel and His Lady: Colonel Eugene Erwin and His Wife Josephine," *Filson Club History Quarterly*, Spring 2001, 208–210.

16. Melba Porter Hay, ed., *The Papers of Henry Clay*, Vol. 10, 881–882.

17. Jefferson Davis to Colonel Hayes, March 18, 1851. UK

18. The Erwin family home in Lexington, Kentucky.

19. Henry Clay to Eugene Erwin, July 19, 1851.

20. Jane Patton Erwin Bell to Andrew Eugene Erwin, March 6, 1853, Special Collections, University of Kentucky Libraries. John Bell was a candidate for president in 1860 but was defeated by Abraham Lincoln.

21. Isaac B. Wall to William H. Russell, "Noticias del Puerto de Monterey," *A Quarterly Bulletin of Historic Monterey*. Issued by the Monterey History and Art Association, March 1958.

22. Author's personal correspondence with the Historian, Monterey Public Library.

23. "Nicaragua Route! Vanderbilt's Independent Line! Fare Reduced! Through Tickets to New York. For San Juan del Sud." *Daily Alta California*, 9 August, 1851 (www.lasuerte.org/artaltaaug9.htm)

24. Edwin P. Hoyt, *The Vanderbilts and Their Fortunes* (New York, 1962), 111–123.

25. E. K. Jamison to Capt. J. H. Blethim, May 16, 1853.

26. "Traveler's Travails," *Daily Alta California*, January 15, 1852 (www.lasuerte.org/artaltajan15.htm).

27. Franklin Walker and G. Ezra Dane, eds., Mark Twain's *Travels with Mr. Brown: Being Heretofore Uncollected Sketches Written by Mark Twain* (New York, 1940), Letters 3–5.

Part II. Mrs. Eugene Erwin

Chapter 4.

1. Mrs. John M. Clay, "Ode to Winter," *Lexington Herald*, January 1904. See Appendix c.

2. An invitation dated June 1853 and a fragment of Josephine's dress were found at Ashland, the Estate of Henry Clay.

3. N. Cannon to Henry Clay, October 4, 1823. Property of William A. LaBach.

4. Electronic Biography of James Patton, University of North Carolina Southern Historical Collection. (http://docsouth.unc.edu/patton/patton.html)

5. William Carroll to Henry Clay, October 10, 1823.

6. Melba Porter Hay, ed., *The Papers of Henry Clay*, Vol. 10, Henry Clay to Lucretia Erwin Cowles, September 14, 1851, 911–912 and author's personal correspondence with William A. LaBach.

7. For more background on the Clay family homes, see Richard M. Bean, "A History of the Henry Clay Properties" (Unpublished, 1980). Copy is on file at Ashland , the estate of Henry Clay.

8. A collection of letters, real estate documents and IOUs between Erwin family members describes James Erwin's transactions.

9. Anne B. Erwin to Henry Clay. April 11, ca. 1832.

10. James Erwin to Henry Clay, December 15, 1835.

11. Remini, *Henry Clay, Statesman for the Union*, 482.

12. James Erwin to William H. Russell, January 12, 1836.

13. Robert Seager, ed., *The Papers of Henry Clay*, Vol. 9, "Bond to John Jacob Astor", 846.

14. Ibid., Henry Clay to Lucretia Hart Clay, February 10, 1843, 800–801.

15. Family Story.

16. Melba Porter Hay, ed., *Supplement to the Papers of Henry Clay*. Henry Clay to John B. Morris, August 12, 1842, 287.

17. Margaret Johnson Erwin to Andrew Eugene Erwin, August 8, 1851, Special Collections, University of Kentucky Library.

18. William A. LaBach, "The Ancestry of James Erwin" (http://members.tripod.com/~labach/erwinanc.htm).

19. Wilcox, *Jackson County Pioneers*, 286–287.

20. Bureau of Land Management – General Land Office Records (http://www.glorecords.blm.gov/PatentSearch/Results.asp?QryId=34179.44).

21. Zaenett Russell to Sarah Russell, March 4, 1855.

22. Georgie Cornwall to Josephine Erwin, ca. 1855.

23. Gustavus Schmidt to Eugene Erwin, June 7, 1861.

24. LaBach, "The Ancestry of James Erwin."

25. Donald R. Hale, "Jackson County and the Civil War," (Jackson County Historical Society), 6–7 and "Major General John C. Frémont" (www.usgennet.org/usa/mo/county/stlouis/fremont.htm).

26. Eugene Erwin to Josephine Erwin, May 14, 1861. UK

27. Brown, "The Colonel and His Lady," 215.

28. Mrs. John M. Clay, *Frank Logan* (New York, 1901), 110–111.

29. Shelby Foote, *The Beleaguered City* (New York, 1963), Reprinted in Modern Library Edition (New York, 1995), 314–327.

30. William LaBach, "The Ancestry of William H. Russell" (http://members.tripod.com/~labach/whrussell.htm)

31. Gustavus Schmidt to Eugene Erwin, December 5, 1861.

32. Brown, "The Colonel and His Lady," 217.

33. Circular written by Col. Eugene Erwin. UK

34. News article in the Scrapbook of Mrs. John M. Clay, ca. July 1862.

35. Jefferson Davis to Col. J. Hayes, Ohio River, March 18, 1851. UK

36. Michael Fellman, *Inside War: The Guerrilla Conflict in Missouri During the American Civil War* (New York, 1989), 92–94, 224.

37. Captain James E. Paine, 6th Missouri Infantry CSA," Henry Clay and The Eventful Life of His Grandson, Eugene Erwin", *Independence Sentinel*, Independence, Missouri, (1883). Anderson Family Scrapbook. Property of William A. LaBach.

38. Family story. Some members of the Clay family were said to be concerned about the lifestyle of Henry Clay's youngest son, John M. Clay and believed that he would benefit from having Josephine Erwin and her family live with him.

39. The Sixth Missouri Infantry, CSA was positioned on the Mississippi River, ten miles northwest of Port Gibson, Mississippi, which is marked today for visitors near the entrance of the Grand Gulf Military Monument Park.

40. Eugene Erwin to Josephine Erwin, February 8, 1863. Special Collections, University of Kentucky Libraries.

41. Mrs. John M. Clay, *Frank Logan*, 154.

42. J. Murdock to Col. Eugene Erwin, undated. UK

Chapter 5.

1. Mrs. John M. Clay, "The Equal Grave," *Lexington Herald*, March 1906. See Appendix c.

2. Foote, *The Beleaguered City*, 314–327.

3. Brown, "The Colonel and His Lady," 226.

4. Ibid., 227.

5. Mrs. John M. Clay, *Uncle Phil*, 227–229.

6. Captain James E. Paine, 6th Missouri Infantry CSA," Henry Clay and The Eventful Life of His Grandson, Eugene Erwin," *Independence Sentinel*, Independence, Missouri, (1883). Anderson Family Scrapbook. Property of William LaBach.

7. Colonel Erwin may have stayed in a large mansion, Anchuca, which served as a temporary hospital near the position of the Sixth Missouri Infantry, CSA during the siege. It is now a bed and breakfast Inn at 1010 First East Street, Vicksburg. (www. AnchucaMansion.com)

8. Mrs. John M. Clay, *Uncle Phil*, 226–227.

9. Capt. James E. Paine, Sixth Missouri Infantry CSA, " Henry Clay and The Eventful Life of His Grandson, Eugene Erwin."

10. Mrs. John M. Clay, *Uncle Phil*, 235–236.

11. W. H. Tunnard, *A Southern Record: The History of the Third Regiment, Louisiana Infantry* (Fayetteville, Ark., 1997), 476.

12. Ibid., 476. The attempt to take Fort Hill was not abandoned. Grant ordered that a new mine be dug under Fort Hill. On the afternoon of July 1, a second explosion completely destroyed the defensive position but Confederate forces were prepared for the attack and no assault was attempted by Federal forces.

13. Confederate Ribbon, June 26, 1863.

14. Tunnard, 258, and Capt. James E. Paine, Sixth Missouri Infantry CSA," Henry Clay and The Eventful Life of His Grandson, Eugene Erwin," *Independence Sentinel*, Independence, Missouri, (1883). Property of William LaBach. The story of the defense of Fort Hill is featured on the audio CD sold at the Vicksburg National Military Park.

15. U. S. Grant, *Personal Memoirs* (1885–86), reprinted by Penguin Books (1999), 312.

16. Sgt. Lucien McDowell to Mrs. Col. Erwin, July 14, 1863. UK

17. Thomas L. Fletcher was a Democrat and strong supporter of President Lincoln. He was elected governor of Missouri, 1865–1869 and was the leader of the state during the Reconstruction period. Lum House was owned by the widow of a wealthy businessman, and faced the Mississippi River at the intersection of Washington and Klein Streets. According to a local story, the widow wrote a letter to Grant accusing Union soldiers of stealing silver and antiques. After Grant left Vicksburg, he ordered an investigation but the house burned before it could be carried out.

18. Capt. James E. Paine, Sixth Missouri Infantry CSA, "Henry Clay and The Eventful Life of His Grandson, Eugene Erwin," *Independence Sentinel*, Independence, Missouri, (1883). According to a family story, Josephine told her grandchildren that she was so upset over Col. Erwin's death that she could not shake hands with General Grant but now felt she made a mistake and should have thanked him for writing the pass and providing free transport to Missouri.

19. Custis Washington to "Mrs. Col. Irwin" (sic), July 23, 1863. UK On July 16, 1863, the Imperial docked in New Orleans eight days out of St. Louis representing the reopening of the Mississippi River to commercial travel. The Erwin family joined the return trip to St. Louis. For a description of the Vicksburg campaign and documentation of the *Imperial's* trip, see *Vicksburg is the Key: The Struggle for the Mississippi River* (Lincoln, Neb., 2003) by William L. Shea and Terrence J. Winschel.

20. Fellman, *Inside War,* 254–255.

21. Ibid.

22. Maj. Gen. John M. Schofield to Mrs. Josephine Erwin, November 3, 1863. UK

23. Henry Clay's son James died in Montreal on January 26, 1864.

24. John M. Clay to Josephine Erwin, December 27, 1863.

25. Mrs. John M. Clay, "Women in the Professions," *Kansas City Star,* June 15, 1903.

26. Family story.

Part III. Josephine Clay, Horsewoman of the Bluegrass

Chapter 6.

1. Mrs. John M. Clay, "Ode to Winter," *Lexington Herald,* January 1904. See Appendix c.

2. Seager, ed., *The Papers of Henry Clay,* Vol. 8, 761.

3. Ibid., 847.

4. Ibid., 308. John M. Clay was listed as a part time student in the class of 1840 at Washington College, now Washington and Jefferson in Washington, Pa.

5. John M. Clay to Mrs. Lucretia H. Clay, May 24, 1841. UK

6. Hay, ed., *The Papers of Henry Clay,* Vol. 10, 213.

7. Cathy C. Schenck, "Descendents of Margaret Wood and Magnolia," March 10, 2004, unpublished note on file at the Keeneland Association Library.

8. Jeff Meyer, "Henry Clay's Legacy to Horse Breeding and Racing," *Register of the Kentucky Historical Society,* Autumn 2002, 479–480.

9. Weeks, ed., *An Historical Account of Racing in the United States,* 168.

10. Deed from Lucretia Clay to John M. Clay for half of blooded stock at Ashland, November 23, 1853.

11. Fayette County Deed Book 29, Page 194.

12. Major Lewinski was a British army officer trained in architecture who moved to Lexington in 1842 and promoted the classical style of English Regency. Henry Clay gave him a commission to design Mansfield, a home for his son Thomas. Lewinski's second marriage was to Henry Clay's grandniece, Mary Louisa Watkins, in 1846. After Lewinski became a member of the family, he was commissioned to design other Clay family homes in the Lexington area. See Clay Lancaster, *Ante-Bellum Houses of the Bluegrass* (Lexington, 1961) and "Major Thomas Lewinski: Emigré Architect in Kentucky," *Journal of Society of Architectural Historians,* December 1952, 13–20.

13. James Clay found the main house at Ashland to be structurally unsound and ordered the house rebuilt on the same foundation using some of the same building materials. The project was designed by Major Lewinski and completed in 1857.

14. The King Library Press, University of Kentucky, *Last Will and Testament of Henry Clay* (1991). Miss Sarah Hall, the long-time Yorkshire housekeeper for the Clay family moved to Ashland on Tates Creek Pike.

15. The entrance to Ashland on Tates Creek Pike was just opposite Tremont Avenue and the road to the house followed Hart Road and Cochran Road. The house, which has been torn down, was replaced by the Chevy Chase Baptist Church at 200 Colony Boulevard.

16. Meyer, "Henry Clay's Legacy to Horse Breeding and Racing," 484.

17. Weeks, ed., *An Historical Account of Racing in the United States,* 168–169.

18. W. S. Vosburgh, *Racing in America* (New York, 1922), 71.

19. William Preston Mangum, II, *A Kingdom for the Horse* (Prospect, Ky., 1999), 115–116, and Jane Fieberts, "Ashland," *The Blood-Horse,* April 24, 1972, 1382.

20. "Death of the Artist Scott," *Turf, Field and Farm*, March 30, 1888, 253 and "Death of Thomas J. Scott," *Live Stock Record*, v. 27, no. 13, March 31, 1888, 198. Keeneland Association Library

21. Mrs. Minor Simpson. Ashland Stock Farm maintained two one-mile tracks side by side—one was about two feet lower than the other, so in wet weather the higher side was used.

22. John M. Clay, "Ashland Stock Book," 1864.

23. Meyer, "Henry Clay's Legacy to Horse Breeding and Racing," 483.

24. Mrs. John M. Clay, *Frank Logan*, 114–134.

25. Fayette County Deed Book 38, Page 313.

26. "Ashland Thoroughbred Stock Farm," Mrs. Minor Simpson.

27. John M. Clay, "Daily Journal," June 10, 1864, Special Collections, University of Kentucky Library.

28. Ashland Stock Book, 1862–1867; and "Iroquois Stud," *Louisville Courier-Journal*, January 13, 1903.

29. Personal correspondence between the curatorial staff at Ashland and the Corcoran Museum, Washington, D. C., October 27, 2004.

30. "Maggie B. B., Queen of the Erdenheim Stud," *The Spirit of the Times*, March 1, 1884, 121–122.

31. "Iroquois Stud," *Louisville Courier-Journal*. For more details about *Maggie B. B.*'s impact on racing, see Floyd Oliver, "Matriarchs of the Turf: The Romance of Maggie B. B.," October 13, 2004 (http://www.equineinfo.com/maggie.htm).

32. Wilkes *Spirit of the Times* (1865), Vol. 13, 231.

33. John M. Clay to Josephine Erwin, August 25, 1864. UK

34. Trustees Deed to Josephine Erwin, State of Missouri, Jackson County, September 5, 1865, Special Collections, University of Kentucky Libraries.

35. Lease Agreement signed by Josephine Erwin, November 14, 1865.

36. John M. Clay, "Daily Journal," Special Collections, University of Kentucky Libraries.

37. Family story.

38. John M. Clay, "Daily Journal," July 7, 1866.

39. Invitation to Paper Wedding , Mr. & Mrs. John M. Clay, July 8, 1867. Ashland, the estate of Henry Clay.

40. Ibid., December 25, 1865.

41. Ibid., July 8, 1866.

42. John M. Clay to Josephine Clay (twenty-nine letters). UK

43. "John M. Clay Dead," *Lexington Herald*, August 11, 1887. John Clay's correspondence mentions St. Pauls.

44. Mrs. John M. Clay, *Sport of Kings*, 23.

45. John M. Clay, "Daily Journal."

46. Mrs. John M. Clay, *Sport of Kings*. See Appendix a.

47. Family story.

48. "Died of Old Age," *New York Times*, March 10, 1889.

49. Fieberts, "Ashland," *The Blood-Horse*, April 24, 1972, 1382.

50. Mrs. Minor E. Simpson, "A Few Memories and a Bit of History."

51. Ibid.

52. Ibid.

53. One other silk racing purse from this era has been located in Kentucky at Churchill Downs, Louisville.

54. Playbill at Ashland, February 21, 1871.

55. John M. Clay to Mrs. Josephine Clay, October 7 (ca. 1869). UK

56. Ibid., October 11, 1870.

57. John M. Clay to Josephine Clay, June 19, 1872. UK

58. John M. Clay to Josephine Clay, June 25, 1872. UK

59. John M. Clay to Josephine Clay, June 30, 1872. UK

60. "First Annual Sale of Yearlings, Property of John M. Clay," June 26, 1863, *Kentucky Gazette*, Lexington, Ky.

61. On May 15, 2004, *Smarty Jones* won the Preakness by eleven and a half lengths and is presently standing at Robert N. Clay's Three Chimneys Farm in Midway, Kentucky.

62. Fieberts, "Ashland," 1382.

63. *Ashland Stock Book*, 1878. UK

64. "John M. Clay Dead," *Lexington Herald*, August, 1887.

65. John M. Clay to Josephine Clay, June 2, 1887. UK

66. "John M. Clay Dead," undated clipping from the *Lexington Herald*. Property of William A. LaBach.

Chapter 7.

1. Mrs. John M. Clay, "Ode to Winter," *Lexington Herald*, October 1904. See Appendix c.

2. Mrs. Minor E. Simpson, "A few Memories, and a Bit of History."

3. Family story.

4. "In Blue Grass Land: The Ashland Thoroughbred Stock Farm Made Famous by Henry Clay Now Conducted by a Woman," *Morning Telegraph* (New York), March 2, 1896.

5. Family story.

6. Simpson Family Scrapbook.

7. See Table 2.

8. After Josephine Clay inherited Ashland Stud, she bred a winner of the Kentucky Derby, the Brooklyn Derby, and the American Derby in Chicago.

9. Mrs. John M. Clay, "Women in the Professions."

10. Mrs. John M. Clay, *What Will the World Say?: A Novel of Every-Day Life; and Only a Woman.*

11. Mrs. John M. Clay, *Some Little of the Angel Still Left* and "Mrs. Clay's Book," *The Thoroughbred Record*, Vol. 46, July-December, 1897.

12. Mrs. John M. Clay, *Uncle Phil.*

13. Mangum, *A Kingdom for the Horse*, 107–113.

14. Mrs. John M. Clay, *Frank Logan.*

15. Mrs. John M. Clay, "The Annual Catalogue of Brood Mares 1899." Keeneland Association Library and Ashland, the Estate of Henry Clay, have examples of the catalogs.

16. "Mrs. Clay, the World's Most Famous Horse Breeder," *The Morning Telegraph*, ca. 1899.

17. Newspaper article ca. 1900.

18. Advertisement for the sale of Ashland's stock in *Turf, Field and Farm* and the statement of Mrs. John M. Clay, "Catalogue of The Ashland Stud," November, 1903. Keeneland Association Library.

19. Ibid.

20. "Horses of Ashland Stud Sold," *New York Times,* November 19, 1903.

Chapter 8.

1. Mrs. John M. Clay, "Autumn," *Lexington Herald*, October 1902. See Appendix c.

2. H. H. Bancroft, "California Pioneer Register and Index 1542–1848," *History of California* (Baltimore, 1964), 316.

3. William LaBach, "The Ancestry of William H. Russell" (http://members.tripod.com/~labach/whrussan.htm).

4. *History of Callaway County*, 269–272.

5. Mrs. Zaenett Russell is buried in Section I, lot 73. The monument has the following inscription written in Latin: "He who follows me walks in the light of life."

6. Family story.

7. John M. Clay , "Daily Journal," List of Farm Workers, ca. 1855.

8. Family story. Major McDowell purchased the old Ashland estate in 1882 and started a second Ashland Farm with trotting horses. His son, Thomas Clay McDowell, raised Thoroughbreds and moved the second Ashland to Woodford County, where he operated the farm until his death in 1935.

9. The quarry is now an abandoned parcel of land on the Delong Road.

10. Mrs. John M. Clay, *Sport of Kings*, 46.

11. Mrs. Sarah S. Young, *Genealogical Narrative of the Hart Family in the United States* (Memphis, 1882), 5–12. Copy on file at Ashland, the Estate of Henry Clay.

12. The deed to Mrs. John M. Clay in April 1905 was from the Second Presbyterian Church for 70 front feet on North Upper Street between Church and Market Streets. The property was resold by Mrs. John M. Clay to C. M. Marshall and Company on October 31, 1912.

13. The historical romance was not published.

14. Probably refers to Alice Roosevelt, President Roosevelt's daughter, who was in the news at this time because of her engagement to Congressman Nicholas Longworth.

15. Mrs. John M. Clay to Mrs. Henry Pindell, March 30, 1905. Property of The Filson Historical Society (Louisville, Kentucky).

16. An invitation and undated newspaper articles from the *Lexington Herald* about Josephine's parties are in the Simpson family scrapbook.

17. The Very Rev. Baker Perkins Lee, Jr., Rector of Christ Church 1901–1905, was a poplar preacher who also conducted a Sunday evening service for the public at Woodland Park Auditorium. It is a family story that Josephine Clay began attending Christ Church after John M. Clay's death and purchased the pew occupied by Henry Clay and his family (marked with a historic plaque), but the practice of owning pews was changed in 1906.

18. Her twenty-seven-year-old granddaughter, Josephine Clay Simpson.

19. Mrs. John M. Clay to Mrs. Henry Pindell, April 23, 1905. Property of The Filson Historical Society.

20. Search of deeds recorded by Mrs. John M. Clay in Fayette County by William A. LaBach.

21. Eva Millar Nourse, *Millar- du Bois Family* (1928).

22. Mrs. John M. Clay, "Research Ledger." Wood Simpson

23. Mrs. John M. Clay, "The Armed Neutrality of Catherine II of Russia," *Lexington Herald*, Undated clipping in the Anderson family scrapbook. Property of William A. LaBach.

24. Mrs. John M. Clay, *Sport of Kings*. See Appendix a.

25. Carter H. Harrison IV to Mrs. Josephine Clay, December 12, 1912. UK. Carter Harrison's father, also Mayor of Chicago was married to Caroline Russell, a descendent of William Russell of Kentucky, Josephine Clay's great uncle.

26. Maitland Allen to Mrs. John M. Clay, Undated.

27. "Brave Missourians Died Defending this Flag" undated news article; "An Historic Flag" undated news article; "Col. Erwin," *Lexington Leader*, June 25, 1913. Property of William A. LaBach.

28. Ibid.

29. Victor Bogaret to Mrs. John M. Clay, March 22, 1919. UK

30. Mrs. Patterson was a descendant of Brig. Gen. William Russell of Virginia.

31. James K. Patterson to Mrs. John M. Clay, March 28, 1920. UK

32. Weeks, ed., *An Historical Account of Racing in the United States*, 169.

33. *Lexington Herald*, March 30, 1920, 12.

Epilogue

1. Eliza H. Clay died in 1825 in Ohio during a family trip to Washington, D. C.

2. Lexington Cemetery files for Section L, Lot 91.

3. Copy of the Will on file at Fayette County Courthouse, #12, March 1916-September 1921.

4. "Mrs. Clay's Estate," *Lexington Herald*, ca. 1920.

5. "Ashland on Tates Creek Pike." Unpublished memorandum of a conversation with Henry Clay Simpson, 1980. Keeneland Association Library.

6. Petition filed in Caddo Parish, Louisiana, No. 23.992 DC, Mrs. Annie CC Watson, et al. vs. Walter Hennig, et al., June 24, 1918.

7. The house is located on the corner of Lakewood Drive and Harmony Hall Lane.

8. Actually, the Simpson family was in excellent health. My father had tuberculosis in the early 1930s and recovered in a sanitarium in North Carolina. By the time he returned to Lexington, he was in excellent health and served as captain of the Lexington Polo Club.

9. William Bagby, "Tell Tales about the IRS," 52–61. An excerpt of the paper is on file at Ashland, the estate of Henry Clay.

10. He also named a road after the Pendennis Club in Louisville Kentucky, and several roads were given family names including Louisiana Avenue, Hart Road and Chenault Road.

11. The survey points of Josephine Clay's properties, as described in the deeds on file at the Fayette County Courthouse, were plotted on a current map of Lexington with DeLorme Topo USA 5.0 software.

12. Loretta Gilliam Brock, *A History of The Woman's Club of Central Kentucky* (Lexington, 1996), 72.

13. Copy of the Will filed November, 1979 at the Fayette County Courthouse.

14. 175 Eastover Drive. See the memorandum of a conversation with Henry Clay Simpson and Jack W. Davis transcribed on June 1, 1978 by Burton Milward. The Ashland training tracks extended along Eastover and Woodlake Way to just beyond Lakewood Drive where the tracks looped around and returned on Colony Boulevard. Keeneland Association Library.

15. John R. Gaines, "Kentucky's Economic Engine," *Lexington Herald-Leader*, February 29, 2004, Section D.

16. "Descendents of Magnolia and Margaret Wood," Cathy C. Schenck, March 10, 2004, on file at Keeneland Association Library. A website (www.pedigreequery.com) can be used to track the pedigree of Thoroughbred horses.

17. Correspondence with Anne Peters, Three Chimneys Farm, Midway, Kentucky, October 19, 2004. The owner of Three Chimneys Farm, Robert N. Clay, is a descendant of a cousin of Henry Clay. He is a past president of the Thoroughbred Club of America.

Selections from the Writing of Josephine Clay

1. Minor editorial changes have been made to the slang dialogue to improve readability.

2. Josephine Clay told her grandchildren that she rode and won a private stakes race for her husband, Mr. John M. Clay. *La Sylphide* was a famous Ashland broodmare, the dam of the four stakes winners—*Semper Fidele, Semper Lex, Semper Rex,* and *Semper Ego. Mat Davis* out of *Star Davis* was an excellent four-mile horse, but according to Josephine was "too willing" and broke down at an early age.

3. At the end of the Civil War, Jerome Clarke was tried, convicted, and hanged in Louisville, Kentucky, on March 15, 1865 before a crowd estimated at 10,000 people.